FLY FISHING

Learn from a Master

December 1990

For Ken,

Happy Chanuka!

Happy Fishing,
It's good to celebrate with you,
Love,

Marilyn & Dietrich

Sports Illustrated Winner's Circle Books

BOOKS ON TEAM SPORTS

Baseball
Football: Winning Defense
Football: Winning Offense
Hockey
Lacrosse
Pitching

BOOKS ON INDIVIDUAL SPORTS

Bowling
Competitive Swimming
Golf
Racquetball
Skiing
Tennis
Track: Championship Running

SPECIAL BOOKS

Canoeing
Fly Fishing
Scuba Diving
Strength Training

Sports Illustrated

FLY FISHING

Learn from a Master

by Bill Mason

Photography by Bill Eppridge
Illustrations by Dick Leyden

Sports Illustrated
Winner's Circle Books
New York

This book is dedicated to my father, Bill Sr., who bought me my first fishing equipment and took me fishing, and to my mother, Mary, who presented a camp that would be the envy of any outfitter

Acknowledgments

To Kathy Gyurkey, for her transcribing help.

To Charlie and Lynn, for their modeling, and to Liza Paschall, for her patience while being photographed performing fishing techniques.

And to all the outfitters, guides, customers, and friends in West Yellowstone, Island Park, and Sun Valley, who, over the course of 19 years, contributed in their own small way to this book.

Special thanks, too, to John Merwin at the Museum of American Fly Fishing, Manchester, Vermont; Farrow Allen and Charlie Lovett at the Fly Fishing Shop, Winooski, Vermont; Bill Alley at the Fly Rod Shop, Stowe, Vermont; Tom Rosenbauer and Howard Steere at Orvis, Manchester, Vermont; Barry Staats and Judy Laurie at The Sporting Gentleman, Media, Pennsylvania; Dan Shields, Steve Sywensky, Dave McMullen, and Bernard Robb at Flyfisher's Paradise, Lemont, Pennsylvania; Joe McMullen at the Spruce Creek Trout Farm, Lemont, Pennsylvania; and Tom Forwood at Eyler's Inc. Fly & Tackle, Bryn Mawr, Pennsylvania.

Picture credits: Pages 16, 19, 20 courtesy of the Museum of American Fly Fishing, Manchester, Vt.; 202 by Dick Leyden; 213 by Fred Arbona Jr.; 192, 201 by Pam Jaspersohn; 209, 214, 215 by David Stoecklein. All drawings by Dick Leyden. All other photographs by Bill Eppridge.

FIRST EDITION   *Designer: Kim Llewellyn*

Library of Congress Cataloging-in-Publication Data

Mason, Bill, 1929–
  Sports Illustrated fly fishing.
  (Sports illustrated winner's circle books)
  Bibliography: p.
  1. Fly fishing. I. Sports illustrated. II. Title.
III. Title: Fly fishing. IV. Series.
SH451.M388   1988   799.1′755   87-36948
ISBN 0-452-26097-3 (pbk.) 88 89 90 91 92 AG/HL 10 9 8 7 6 5 4 3 2 1

Contents

FLY FISHING

Learn from a Master

Introduction:
Why Fish the Fly?

Why people pursue fly fishing rather than other fishing methods has probably been the most debated question concerning the sport. There is no definitive answer to this question. One person's attraction may not be another's, but certain common bonds—a love of the outdoors, a passion for understanding various species, and a patience born of deep feeling for the beautiful complexity of the sport—unite all fly fishermen.

Under my father's tutelage I began as an angler when I was six. I have fished the fly every season since, and my love for it continues to grow unabated. I can't seem to get enough of fly fishing, and when the season for it ends in Sun Valley, where I live, I find myself packing my gear to fish the fly in other parts of the world. What is it about the sport that draws us so completely to it?

Essentially, fishing as a pastime is a game, and the sport of fly fishing is its pinnacle. In all games we have an opponent and in the sport of fishing the opponent becomes the fish itself. Because this incredible adversary neither lies nor cheats but rather reacts upon its own instincts for survival, the intrigue of angling for it on equally honest terms runs deep.

For most people, the fishing game starts at an early age, simplified in form and technique. A fishing pole, a plain line, a pocket full of hooks and sinkers, and a coffee can filled with night crawlers or grasshoppers generally starts the game in motion. But after awhile, something begins to happen. Through observation of fish habits and, perhaps, an inherent desire to make the game more complex, the angler slowly turns his attention toward the fly rod and the insects so attractive to the fish. By becoming a fly fisherman, the angler discovers he has entered a world and a game that can consume him for the rest of his life. Dealing as it does with Nature and her creatures, the sport of fly fishing is always variable, never constant, and the angler alert to its variations learns

11

The author practicing what he preaches on Idaho's famed Silver Creek.

something new on every outing. Indeed, the daily subtle changes that the angler faces are one reason why the appeal of fly fishing is so great for so many people.

The knowledge gained through fly fishing holds special appeal, too. A good fly fisherman finds himself becoming an amateur ichthyologist studying fish, a hydrologist analyzing water, an entomologist identifying insects, and a meteorologist recognizing weather patterns. All these subjects require a lifetime of attention and study, but the quest for knowledge is one of the sport's continuing attractions.

Fly fishing has often been described as an art form. In other methods of fishing, the weight of lure, plug, or bait propels the cast. In fly fishing, the motion of the rod casts the fly line and the line, in turn, the fly. Placing the fly exactly where it should go requires precision and skill—and more delicacy and "touch" than does any other casting method. In fly fishing, as we shall see, the presentation of the fly—that is, the manner in which it is laid on the water and made to act—is at least as important as the choice of the fly. The "chuck and chance" technique so often characteristic of other casting methods won't work for the fly fisherman. He must put in the hours to perfect both his casting and his presentation techniques.

In other fishing methods (lower illustration), the weight of the lure, plug, or bait propels the cast. In fly fishing (upper illustration), the motion of the rod casts the fly line, which, in turn, casts the fly.

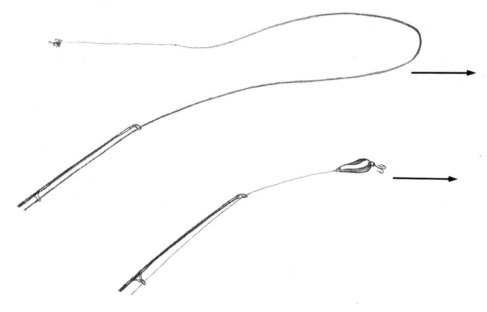

Most fly fishermen ultimately become more interested in the method than in the final outcome of fishing the fly. They rapidly acquire a quiet admiration for the fish they hunt, and they come to realize that to kill it is to kill the very thing that keeps them coming back to the water. It becomes more important that the fish survive to be hooked again—and again—for it is in the hunting, stalking, and deceiving that the satisfaction lies, not in the keeping and killing.

Fly fishing is not an especially "physical" sport. All it really requires is a desire to learn. Because it actually sparks that desire, fly fishing's appeal is broad, and women and children of all ages can and do become equal participants with men, and sometimes even prove to be the better anglers.

Fly fishing is an endlessly aesthetic sport. Roderick Haig-Brown neatly summed up its appeal for any angler, young or old, male or female, in his book *A River Never Sleeps:* "I still don't know why I fish or why other men fish except that we like it and it makes us think and feel. But I do know that if it were not for the strong, quick life of rivers, for their sparkle in the sunshine, for the cold greyness of them under the rain and the feel of them about my legs as I set my feet hard down on rocks or sand or gravel, I should fish less often. A river is never quite silent, it can never of its very nature be quite silent. It is never quite the same from one day to the next. It has its own life and its own beauty and the creatures it nourishes are alive and beautiful also. Perhaps fishing is for me only an excuse to be near rivers. If so I'm glad I thought of it."

This book has been written not only for novice or entry-level fly fishermen but also for those fishermen who have attained, or wish to attain, an intermediate's grasp of the sport. *It is not a book on advanced technique, theories, and application,* but rather a book that specifically deals with detailed and pertinent information that should be known by any fly fisherman. In addition to the basic information, such as fly casting, entomology, and various fly fishing techniques, I will touch upon the use of the fly rod for such fish as bass, steelhead, and salmon, as well as saltwater species.

In fly fishing, as in any other sport, misconceptions abound, and this book is intended in part to clear up some of them.

More than anything, this book is a primer on fly fishing. If reading it stimulates you to learn even *more* about the sport, then it will have accomplished its purpose.

—Bill Mason
Sun Valley, Idaho

1

The History of Fly Fishing

The history of fly fishing has been long and fascinating—a saga of technological innovation and conceptual development with its own literature and cast of characters. Over the years fly fishing has evolved from a simple pastime to something of a science and an art form. Numerous individuals, each in his own small way, have been responsible for advancing the craft. It's very possible that we ourselves, through our own love of the sport, might make a contribution to its future.

Ancient Oriental writings indicate that 4,000 years ago, during the Shang Dynasty in China, an artificial fly was used to catch fish. Despite that reference, most historians place the beginnings of the sport in Macedonia (northern Greece), at about the fourth century B.C.—more than 2,200 years ago. The ancient writer Aelian (230 to 170 B.C.) wrote that the Macedonians observed an insect hovering near and over water, that the insect did not resemble a common wasp, a house fly, or a bee, but, as Aelian said, it has something of each of these. He described the Macedonians' feathered imitation of the insect: two feathers from a cock's wattle fastened to a hook wrapped in red or crimson wool. Aelian also explained the use of a very long rod to which a line and a fly were attached, to deceive "a speckled fish" that lived in those waters.

These early writings merely describe how humans were fishing a fraudulent fly. It was not until 1496 that the first basic "how-to" book of fly fishing appeared. Called *The Boke of St. Albans,* this volume was a group of instructional manuals, providing instruction in such gentlemanly sports as fishing, falconry, and hunting.

The fishing portion was written by Dame Juliana Berners, at the time Prioress of the Nunnery of Sopewell, near St. Albans, England, and was entitled "Treatyse of Fysshynge wyth an Angle." Berners covered such things as mate-

Frontispiece to the original edition of *The Boke of St. Albans* (1496). The section in the book titled "Treatyse of Fysshynge wyth an Angle," attributed to Dame Juliana Berners, is widely considered the first how-to text on fly fishing.

rial for rods (the middle of green hazel; the top of blackthorn, crabtree, medlar, or juniper; the butt of willow, hazel or aspen . . .) and lines (horsehair), the best time of day to fish and, most important, 12 flies that should be used. She even included a simple code of conduct for fishing on private land, and with other anglers.

In 1653, an Englishman who was to become the patron saint of fishing, Izaak Walton, published his *The Compleat Angler.* Walton was not exactly an advocate of fly fishing—the book dealt chiefly with bait fishing—but he did give a current description of the sport as it was then practiced. *The Compleat Angler* was enormously popular, rivaling the Bible in sales. Six editions were published, and it was not until the last of these that Walton asked a close fishing companion, Charles Cotton, to write a special section on fly fishing, which was published in 1676.

Cotton, a true specialist, described in detail how to taper and weave together the various types of horsehair to form a line for rods that were 18 feet long. Most important, he provided a full description of some 65 different flies that should be used over the expanse of an entire fishing year. This may be the first recognition that insect activity changed monthly, requiring a corresponding change in flies.

Although the 1700s did bring other works, it was not until the early 19th century that the sport began to change significantly. Equipment became more advanced. Literature revealed ever more precise technique and insect-fly relationship. Most important, the sport was beginning to grow in North America.

The patron saint of fishing, Izaak Walton.

Because skills and information had become more highly developed, this period
has become known as "the scientific era."

Up until that time, most flies were used with little regard as to what they imitated. A few inquisitive souls did ponder why certain flies worked at certain times, but they were not prominent. In 1836, Alfred Ronalds wrote *The Fly Fisher's Entomology,* which is probably the first book to explain the various aquatic insects and their importance to trout. Ronalds not only categorized some of the insects that occupied the streams in England, he also gave some descriptions about how to imitate them. He did his work so well that even today the book is a valued reference for those anglers lucky enough to have found it.

Heretofore, most fly fishing was done with a wet or subsurface fly. That was only natural, since the hooks were heavy and the materials water absorbent. At the same time, actual surface feeding by fish was not going unnoticed by the observant Frederick M. Halford, an Englishman who was to perfect the techniques and flies that led directly to the dry fly fishing of today. His books, *Floating Flies and How to Dress Them* (1886), and *Dry Fly Fishing in Theory and Practice* (1889), brought him a legion of followers. In fact, Halford's popularity was so great that for many of the fishermen of his time dry fly fishing became the *only* way to fish.

Halford had a philosophical counterpart, G.E.M. Skues, who felt that if surface feeding was absent one should not simply retire to his pint of ale. Instead, said Skues, in his book, *Minor Tactics of the Chalk Stream* (1910), precisely tied subaquatic forms should be used to increase the angler's opportunities. Both Halford and Skues were monumental figures in their sport, one through his contributions to dry fly fishing and the other through his serious revisions of nymph techniques (that is, fishing with patterns that imitate insects' immature stages).

The 1800s also brought important changes in equipment. Lines changed from horsehair to silk. The crude reels (or winches, or winds, as they were then called) that had been in use in the late 1700s became outmoded. Now that anglers were storing and casting line, a full-functioning reel became a necessity. By the end of the 19th century, the reel had evolved into a prototype of the reels we use today.

The most significant advance in equipment was the development of the bamboo fly rod—and it was an American, not an English, innovation. In 1845, a Pennsylvania violin maker, Samuel Phillippe, laminated split segments of bamboo together to create a strong, flexible rod with casting qualities superior to those of any material of the past. Bamboo completely changed the structure of the sport. Fishermen were charmed by the ease and fluidity of motion made

A set of fine old fly-fishing equipment, from the 1860s and '70s. Note the lightweight spoked reel and hand-wound rod grip.

possible by bamboo. It was such a giant leap forward that bamboo rods revolutionalized the sport forever.

From a historical standpoint, the arrival of fly fishing in North America during the 19th century was probably the sport's single most important development. Toward the end of the 1700s, the American colonist could finally lay down his pick, plow, hammer, and musket long enough to devote himself to pastimes more for leisure than for survival. Fishermen began casting flies on American waters, and with the diversity of waters available, improvements in technique and equipment came rapidly. Once purely the domain of the Englishman, fly fishing was about to enter into what I call the "American Period."

In the years that followed, North American names became preeminent in the sport. Hiram Leonard, who constructed his first six-strip bamboo rods in Bangor, Maine, in 1870, was probably foremost among the new American innovators. Many of the people who worked with Leonard went on to make their own contributions to the art of rod building. F.E. Thomas was certainly one of these, as were Hiram and Loman Hawes, E.H. Edwards, and E.F. Payne, whose rods were cherished and whose skill was later perpetuated by his son Jim

As this 1872 Currier & Ives print shows, fly-fishing garb and equipment were different back then, but the pleasure of hooking a big fish was the same.

up through World War II. Other craftsmen who developed rods in the 1920s, '30s, and '40s were Dickerson, Garrison, Gillum, Halstead and Young, and Winston and Powell. Today the rodmaking craft perfected by these men still flourishes under the names Orvis, Thomas and Thomas, and the very fine G.H. Howells.

At the turn of the century, America began to create its own fishing legends. One of these was Theodore Gordon, from the Catskills of New York, who is affectionately referred to as the "Father of American Fishing." A sickly, small, frail man, Gordon corresponded regularly with Halford in England concerning the tying and fishing of the dry fly. Gordon's waters, however, were much swifter, and the hatches different, than on the trout streams of England. He quickly developed his own imitations of hatches occurring on his beloved stream, the Neversink, in upstate New York. He invented the famous Gordon Quill (a.k.a. Quill Gordon), which is still used today. He was a very private man, and little is known about his personal life, but to the fishing public he remains the single most significant American in the history of the sport.

By World War I, North American anglers were developing their own

The man often called "the father of American fly fishing," Theodore Gordon.

fishing skills and publications. The American counterparts of Halford and Skues were George LaBranche, who in 1914 published *The Dry Fly and Fast Water,* and Edward Ringwood Hewitt, who gave us *Telling on the Trout* (1926) and *Better Trout Streams* (1931). LaBranche's books became American classics, supplanting the British texts (which were based on the flat chalk streams of England) and speaking to the demands of the fast-moving waters of New York's Catskills and Pennsylvania's Broadheads. Hewitt was fascinated by the ecology of trout and trout streams, and, in fact, did some of the initial research in the field. He also was the inventor of the very famous "bivisible" flies, which were tied as searching flies, or nondescript patterns used when feeding activity was absent.

Other books would become equally important. *Trout Flies* by Preston Jennings came out in 1935, and probably the most important "bible" produced for the American fly fisherman was *Trout,* by Ray Bergman, in 1938. I read it as a boy, and from it I gleaned much of my early understanding of both the fish and the sport.

Before the Second World War, many other people, too numerous to name, contributed to the lore of fishing, both nationally and internationally. The sport had now reached the proportions of a national pastime, with practitioners in every walk of life. But war would take the angler to the trenches of Europe and the ocean beaches of the Pacific, away from his beloved streams. The war's impact on fly fishing would not come in more conceptual innovation, but indirectly through research into new synthetic materials. These amazing materials would change the sport forever. After the war, we entered into what I call the "Synthetic Period."

Up until this time, bamboo was the principal material used for fly rods. Other materials were tried, but bamboo remained the standard. The war brought us fiberglass. Introduced in 1946, it was destined to put a serious dent in the bamboo rod market. Just as bamboo had once supplanted several other fibers as the choice for fishing rods, fiberglass now supplanted bamboo.

Concurrently with fiberglass rods came the development of synthetic fly lines, which would alter the sport immeasurably. Until the mid-1950s silk, drastically refined since the early 1800s, was still the best fly fishing line money could buy. Unfortunately silk was not durable. And, to say the least, it was troublesome, because it had to be dressed before each fishing outing. A company in Midland, Michigan, Scientific Angler, developed a method of applying and tapering polyvinyl chloride to a Dacron-type core to produce a trouble-free floating line that made silk fly lines nonexistent almost overnight.

In addition to new lines, the 1950s brought extruded nylon materials to replace silk gut material for leaders. Gone forever were the moistening tins that the otherwise stiff gut leader required for elasticity.

Postwar writing on fly fishing also turned a corner. For the most part, the Depression-era fishermen were not necessarily entomology-minded, although they did understand the relationship of insect to fish. Their fly boxes usually contained a series of patterns that they knew, or had heard, worked. In a general way, these patterns simulated various flies upon which trout were known to feed, but they were not necessarily oriented to the aquatic insects actually at hand. More precise information and imitations were necessary, and the new literature responded with a more exacting approach to insects and flies.

An early significant work, *Streamside Guide to Naturals and Their Imitations* (1947), by Art Flick, although written for the Catskills streams in and around the author's beloved Schoharie, described both natural mayflies and the patterns used to imitate them.

In 1950, Vincent Marinaro wrote *A Modern Dryfly Code*. Its most significant lessons for the fly fishing world centered on the trout's "window" (that is, his range of vision), his feeding selectivity, and the significance of a fly's silhouette as it appears to the trout. His greatest creation was the "thorax-wing style" fly, so widely used today.

The first book to describe the hatches in U.S. ecosystems, not only of the Western mountains and the Rockies, but also those of the well-fished Eastern and Midwestern streams, was *Matching the Hatch,* by Ernest Schwiebert. This, the first of many groundbreaking studies that Schwiebert has produced, was completed in 1955 while the author was still an undergraduate. For all anglers, it remains one of the most significant books on the mayfly, as well as other aquatic organisms and their imitations.

The late 1950s and the 1960s were not without their own how-to books. If Ray Bergman's *Trout* was the standard text for pre-war fishermen, Joe Brooks' books carried the banner for the next two decades. I had the privilege to guide Joe and his lovely wife, Mary, in the years before his death. He was not only a great fisherman but a fine gentleman. His *Complete Book of Fly Fishing* (1958) discussed all aspects of trout fly fishing, but might have been the first significant treatment of saltwater fly fishing, of which he is today considered a pioneer. In 1972, Joe Brooks published his final book, *Trout Fishing,* still widely used as a guide for the novice angler.

Fly tying also became popular during this period, even to the average fisherman. In 1951, William Blades, perhaps the greatest fly tying talent since the 1930s, published *Fishing Flies and Fly Tying.* Blades tied flies beautifully and creatively. His flies had an exactness of appearance unlike anything seen up until that time.

This was an important period for anglers throughout the world. A fundamental transition was about to take place in how fishermen viewed their sport and treated the stream environment. Writers like Schwiebert and Marinaro had planted the seeds for greater appreciation of precise entomology, which now not only sprouted but exploded. In the 1970s, we entered what I call the "Enlightenment Period."

Whether the book *Selective Trout,* published in 1971 by Dr. Carl Richards and Doug Swisher, created the attitudes of the 1970s can be debated, but without question their work made a greater impression than any previous book. *Selective Trout* changed the consciousness of the everyday fisherman, as well as instructional technique promulgated today. The great significance of the work lay in its treatment of entomology and fish selectivity, leading to the introduction of a new selection of flies designed to imitate specific species of mayflies. The new patterns, called "no hackles," have become the standard for selective trout on selective water. Critics question the originality of no-hackles, pointing out that Berners and Walton had created similar, albeit cruder, patterns hundreds of years earlier. In any case, the no-hackles re-formed the conventional patterns into more precise imitations of known species of mayfly.

Other insect-oriented books followed this landmark work. Not only the mayfly, but also the stonefly and the caddisfly, became the subject of whole volumes. *Hatches,* by Bob Nastasi and Al Caucci; *Caddisflies,* by Gary LaFontaine; *Stoneflies,* by Carl Richards, Doug Swisher and Fred Arbona, Jr., and *Mayflies, the Angler and the Trout,* by Fred Arbona, Jr. are a few examples of the books that have made a lasting impact.

The 1970s also produced a single replacement for all the previous how-to books. *Trout,* by Ernest Schwiebert, two volumes and some 1,700 pages in

With their outstanding strength and light weight, graphite rods are preferred today by most anglers.

length, is monumental in its depth concerning all subjects of fly fishing.

This period has not been without its advances in equipment. In 1973, the introduction of graphite as a material for fly rods rendered all other types passé. Graphite rods were extraordinarily light and strong, and they retained the best qualities of their forebears. Boron rods, introduced in the 1980s, are considered a new advance, but they do not now represent the kind of departure from past limitations that graphite offered. Today, new directions in graphite appear to be setting the directions of fly rods for the future.

In general, though, the question of the future of the sport is open to speculation. New techniques will always be developed. I feel that advances will not necessarily be conceptual but will come about because of still more wonderous synthetic materials from which more durable and exacting fly imitations can be made. I also foresee the use of transparent hooks to further refine the optical illusions we work so hard to create, as well as synthetic material for rods, reels, and lines. Who knows? We might even develop the indestructible wader!

But product development will be of secondary importance to our concern for the streams and waterways that make our sport possible. As man encroaches upon the environment and industrialization continues, with consequences ranging from organic pollution to acid rain, anglers will have to step forward and take action to preserve the sport of fishing. This may be the greatest challenge to the angler yet.

Now that we have seen where the sport has been and where it may be headed, it's time for you to get involved. Your first step is to learn about the basic equipment necessary to perform your duties as a fly fisherman.

2

Equipment

The appeal of fly fishing provides an interesting study in tastes. For most, including myself, it is the satisfaction of catching fish. For others, it is the pleasure of fly tying or equipment collecting—or just plain casting. Whatever the area of one's interest, though, the elegance of the gear adds to the mystery and beauty of the sport.

Unfortunately, because rods come in a full array of sizes and flexes, reels in different designs and dimensions, lines in different densities and tapers, and leaders in different diameters, the novice angler can easily become confused about which equipment to buy. Then, too, there's the matter of price: Fly fishing equipment can range from the suspiciously cheap to the outrageously expensive. In general, price reflects quality. You don't need to spend the family fortune on equipment, but you shouldn't skimp on it either. The better the equipment you buy, the longer it should last and the more enjoyment it can give you. Many fine old reels and rods, passed down through generations, are still functional today because the quality was good when purchased.

In short, when buying gear, go for the best you can afford. You won't be disappointed.

FLY RODS

A fly rod is to the fisherman what a hammer is to the carpenter, a club to the golfer and a racket to the tennis player: a basic tool. Centuries ago in England, where modern fly fishing got its start, fly rods were made from various species of either indigenous or imported woods. Because in those days flies were dabbed, not cast, rods were enormously long, sometimes 18 or 20 feet. Fly

Always buy your gear—particularly rods and reels—from a reputable fly-fishing dealer.

casting, or "delivering" the fly, would come later and rod lengths would shorten considerably.

Today, fly fishing rods come in various materials, with bamboo, fiberglass, graphite and boron the substances used most often. Each has its own qualities and drawbacks, so before purchasing rods made of any of these materials, you'd be wise to learn about each.

Split Bamboo

Split bamboo or split cane is one of the oldest fly rod materials still in use. First developed in 1845 and later commercialized by Hiram Leonard in the 1870s, bamboo is still considered one of the finest materials for fly rods and the one against which all subsequent rod-making substances have been measured. It is both strong and durable, and in casting, it exhibits a smoothness and "feel" that has not been perfectly duplicated even by our most modern synthetic materials.

The basic design and "lay-up" of the rod has not changed dramatically in a hundred years. The first rods were made from Calcutta cane, later to be replaced by Tonkin cane, from the plant *Arundaria amabilis,* grown in the Kwangsi Province of southern China.

To construct a cane rod today, the rod maker splits a culm or stock of bamboo into strips, planing and tapering each one into a long triangular shape. He then laminates or glues the strips together to form the rod. Early rods were of three- or four-strip construction, but most modern versions follow Hiram

Bamboo rods.
Though beautiful and functional, they can also be heavy and expensive.

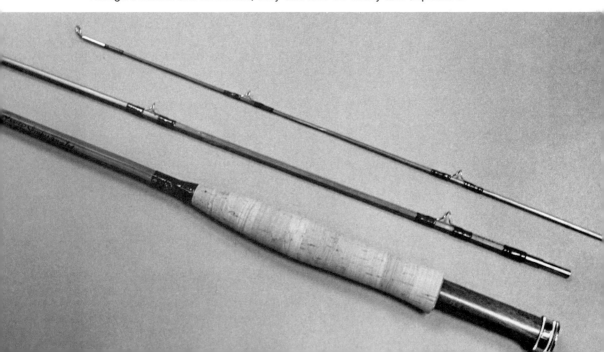

Leonard's six-strip derivation. Aside from the guides and fittings, the only difference 100 years has made is that most of today's rod makers use synthetic glues for the laminations and sophisticated mitering saws rather than hand planes for more precise cuts.

As beautiful and functional as bamboo rods are, they do have their drawbacks. Because of the nature of the material, the rods are heavy, especially compared to today's synthetic models. Bamboo rods more than eight-and-a-half feet long can be tiring to use over a full day's casting. In addition, there is the expense. A quality bamboo rod fetches about $500 or more, putting it somewhat out of the budget range of many fishermen.

Fiberglass

Synthetic fiberglass and resins were actually discovered in the early 1900s, but not until World War II did fiberglass come into its own as a material for making fishing rods. While doing work in tubular fiberglass research for the military, Dr. Art Howald happened to break his bamboo fly rod. He adapted a crudely developed tubular fiberglass piece to replace the tip portion—and immediately recognized the great potential of his casual experiment. A few years later, in 1946, the Shakespeare Rod Company developed the "Wonder Rod," the first fiberglass rod to be offered commercially. These initial fiberglass products were expensive, but as production techniques were refined, prices dropped drastically, making a rod affordable to all anglers. Fiberglass soon outsold even the less expensive bamboo models, and the sport was flooded with new anglers.

Fiberglass fly rods are constructed of a woven fiberglass cloth impregnated with resins, rolled around a highly machined core called a mandrel, then wrapped with a cellophane material to hold the shape. The resin-impregnated cloth is cured in a special oven, the mandrel is afterwards removed, and the blank is sanded and finished. The addition of guides and fittings completes the rod.

The advantages of fiberglass are many: Besides being inexpensive, the rods are lightweight and extremely strong. For some applications, such as saltwater, they are still preferred to any other material. Fiberglass has some disadvantages, but they are fairly minor. Because of the power and flex recoverability (stiffness) inherent in the material, rods designed for very light fly lines are difficult to produce. Furthermore, fiberglass has a tendency to oscillate or vibrate during and after the cast and thus has never truly matched the smoothness of bamboo.

Just as fiberglass rods were becoming highly refined, the seventies brought a new material that would displace both bamboo and fiberglass—graphite.

Graphite

In 1973, I had the opportunity to cast the first prototype fly rod made of carbon graphite fiber by the Fenwick Rod Company of Westminster, California. That first experience was both enlightening and mystifying. The rod was as light as a feather, yet so incredibly powerful that a full 90-foot fly line could be cast with virtually no effort. What was this magic material, I wondered, and how was it made?

Graphite is a synthetic fiber—chemists call it polyacrylonitrile—that is subjected to a series of heat treatments, starting at 200 degrees and ending at about 2800, finally, in an oxygen-free environment. Under these conditions, instead of burning, the fibers carbonize, then graphitization takes place forming crystals, which are stretched into fibers. The fibers are then laid side by side, and wrapped on a mandrel similar to that used for fiberglass rods. The result is an enormously strong, lightweight material with a power-to-weight ratio far superior to that of any other material that has ever been used in fly rod construction.

Graphite rod construction. Here, sheets of graphite await wrapping around aluminum mandrels. After the graphite is cured, the mandrel is removed, and the hollow graphite blank is fitted with various rod hardware.

The first graphite rods were almost too powerful for everyday trout fishing, but were perfect for salmon and steelhead angling, which require long casts. The recovery flex factor was so great that early rods did not fish especially well with fine leaders; they constantly separated fly and leader from the fish when the angler tried to strike and set the hook.

In order to dissipate this power, the next generation of graphite rods were made lengthier than those of conventional fiberglass, adding flexibility and softness to the rod. Today, further refinement has resulted in short rods that will also handle very light fly lines.

The first of the graphites were very expensive (at least by 1974 dollars), but the rods' quickly won popularity has brought the price of many down from the $250 range to the $60 range. Indeed, graphite has generally replaced fiberglass as the fly rod of choice. Because graphite has come the closest to duplicating the feel of bamboo, it has also made inroads into the traditional bamboo market. For my money, a good graphite rod is a sensible—though not essential—investment.

Boron

With the introduction and development of graphite, manufacturers quickly moved on to explore other new synthetics, particularly boron. As a material for fly rods, boron, although exotic, has not enjoyed the general acceptance that graphite received when it appeared on the market.

The fiber used in boron fly rods is made from a compound, deposited as a vapor upon ultra-fine tungsten wire. The resulting filament is not only delicate and light but also extremely strong. The strength-to-weight ratio of the material has allowed manufacturers to reduce the diameter of a fly rod by about 20 percent, resulting in a much lighter rod.

So far, the advantages of boron have been demonstrated only in the rods used on big rivers or for working sizable sea-run fish, such as steelhead or salmon. Because the material is so much more powerful even than graphite, it has not as yet been successful in rods designed to handle very light lines. Also, to date, boron rods are uniformly expensive (between $375 and $450).

Without question, graphite, boron, and very possibly other as yet undiscovered Space Age materials will be used to make the fly rods of the future. With each new development comes a more powerful yet lighter, more responsive rod. I can't wait to see what will be next.

ROD LENGTHS AND ROD FUNCTIONS

The standard medium-sized trout rod purchased today is generally eight to eight-and-a-half feet long and throws a six-weight line (more on line weights later), and it is against these variables that you can choose lighter and shorter or heavier and longer equipment. If you fish primarily small or delicate water (narrow, shallow streams or still pools), then a rod of seven-and-a-half to eight feet, throwing a four-weight or five-weight line, may be appropriate. If your interest lies with bigger water (wider, deeper streams), bass fishing, lake fishing, and/or light steelhead fishing, a rod in the eight-and-a-half to nine-and-a-half foot range, throwing a seven- to ten-weight line, should be used. And, finally, if you are mainly after steelhead and saltwater fish, a rod of nine-and-a-half to ten feet that throws an 11-, 12-, or 13-weight line is a must. Note: Today, rods that throw three, two, or even one-weight lines are also available, though not terribly practical for most fishing situations.

This is only a general guide. As you begin to shop for equipment, you'll find that manufacturers make a full array of rods and lengths, with most being capable of throwing several different line sizes.

Parts of a Fly Rod

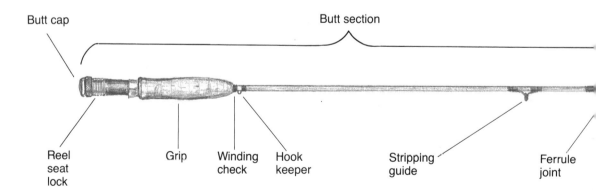

Length and Line Specifications on a Fly Rod

A rod's length and line specifications are usually marked either above the handle or on the butt. This three oz. rod is eight feet long and designed to throw a seven-weight line.

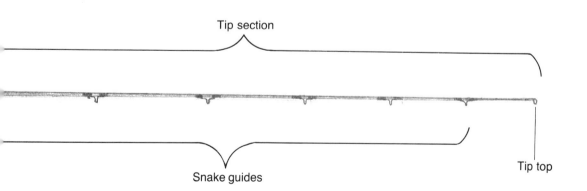

Tip section

Snake guides

Tip top

FLY REELS

There is evidence in fly fishing literature that fly reels constructed of hardwoods were in use in England in the late 1700s. But it wasn't until well into the 1800s that the fly reel's development really took off. Early reels were made of wood, evolving to solid brass, and were quite different from today's reels, which are fashioned from alloys of aircraft aluminum or graphite.

To many people the fly reel has just one function, to store line. Granted, storage is a primary function, but a quality modern reel has other features that also should be considered when shopping for the right model. The fly reel you

Parts of a Fly Reel

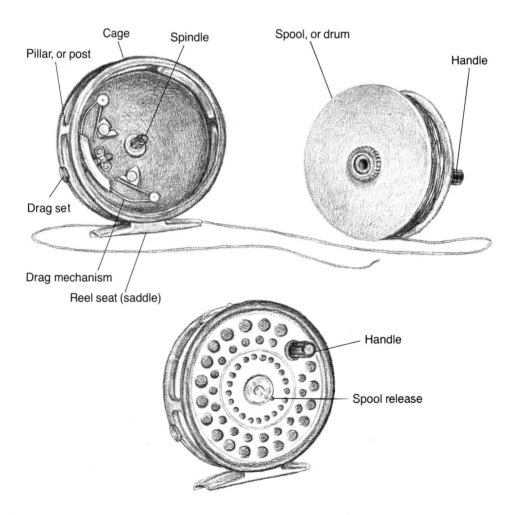

Cage

Spindle

Spool, or drum

Pillar, or post

Handle

Drag set

Drag mechanism

Reel seat (saddle)

Handle

Spool release

choose should have an *adjustable drag,* enabling you to set the tension commensurate with the leader you are using and the size of fish you intend to catch. The drag function also prevents the spool from overrunning and letting out too much line, eliminating backlash problems.

In addition to lightness and an adjustable drag, there are other features that should be considered in a fly reel. Fly reel spools should be perforated. Although not essential to the reel's performance, this feature does help to evaporate and eliminate moisture when the line is stored on the reel, and to reduce the reel's weight. Some reels come with either an exposed or a flanged rim on the spool itself. This can aid the fisherman when he wants to "palm" the reel (place the palm of his hand over it) for additional drag. Although they work very nicely, I have found them to be rather temperamental, for if they are dropped on a hard surface they have a tendency to either dent or misalign themselves, which causes rubbing on the reel cage. Finally, any reel you buy should have available additional spools that fit your particular model. There is nothing worse than buying a reel and not being able to find extra spools when additional fly lines are needed, and these days, with enormous numbers of reels being introduced and discontinued, this problem is more severe than I can ever remember.

Fly rods don't generally wear out; they are much more likely to get broken underfoot or in car doors. That is not the case with fly reels, however. Inexpensive reels with plastic internal parts can wear out. Consequently, to avoid having to buy replacement reels, it's better to spend the extra money for a good reel initially. Good reels aren't cheap—generally $100 to $200—but the best are likely to last a lifetime.

There is a wide assortment of fly reels available, with widely varying prices. Let's examine the different types.

Single Action Flyreels

The single action reel is the most popular type of fly reel on the market today. It is the one I recommend to all anglers, because of its ease and reliability. "Single action" refers to the reel's one-to-one ratio: One revolution of the handle turns the spool one revolution. The construction is simple. A cage houses the simple drag mechanism, and the spool or drum is inserted in it. All single action fly reels can be adjusted and mounted on the rod for either right-hand or left-hand winding. Additional spools can and should be purchased to accommodate different types of fly lines. Also, various reel sizes are available, enabling you to balance the reel to the rod and to allow for greater line capacity when you are pursuing large fish.

Single-action fly reels.

The advantage of the single action reel is its simplicity and generally its lightness. The main weakness is its susceptibility to wear, especially among the cheaper models. Remember, good ones cost more but they can last a lifetime.

The Automatic Fly Reel

The automatic fly reel has been around for years. Often called "the reel of the President," because Warren G. Harding used it, its design features a coiled spring system surrounding a center spindle. The spring is tightened either by a screw cap or by stripping line off the reel. Instead of turning a handle, the angler activates a trigger, which releases the spring, retrieving the line.

This reel has some strong advocates—and some serious faults. It is heavier than a single action reel, and the spool has a limited capacity, which prevents a fisherman from using additional fly line backing with his fly line (more on lines and backing in a moment). Because of the spring tension, the fine drag setting (needed to prevent fine leaders from breaking when a fish is on) is almost nonexistent. And because the spool is not easily removed, the reel lacks the useful interchangeable spool function. I used an automatic reel once and the experience convinced me that single action reels are better and more versatile.

The Multiplying Fly Reel

The multiplying fly reel is essentially a single action reel with added gears that allow you to reel up line at a rate up to two-and-a-half times faster than with a single action reel. It is not especially popular for normal trout fishing, but it can be a real help to those regularly casting long distances. The disadvantages? The gearing system adds extra weight and bulk, and in the cheaper models, the gears' levers sometimes bind up when a large fish is hooked. That happened once to a client of mine when he hooked a very large rainbow. The reel froze and the leader and fly line instantly separated. I have been wary of multiplying reels ever since.

A multiplying fly reel.

Saltwater Reels

When you venture into salt water you need a rugged reel because of the size and strength of the fish. Saltwater fish are very strong, and a reel with a sophisticated drag system to handle their devastating runs is called for. Most saltwater reels are hand machined of barstock aluminum to infinitely precise tolerances. The drag is generally a pressure type, much like that used in automotive disc brakes, and is designed to withstand the heat buildup that occurs when the line spins off the spool at high speeds.

There are many new saltwater reels on the market, and most are expensive—$350 to $450. But if you are earnestly going to fish salt water you will need one, and, believe me, it's money well spent.

Typical saltwater fly reels.

ROD-REEL BALANCE

Now that you know something about rods and reels, it is time to choose an appropriate reel size to meet your fishing needs. Regardless of your chosen equipment, the most important selection factor is balance. First, you need a rod to fit the style of fishing you wish to do and, second, a reel that balances to that rod. Balancing the rod and reel requires no mathematical formula. Mount a reel on a rod and hold it in your hand. If it balances nicely with the rod remaining level, you have a match. Remember that adding fly line to the reel will increase the weight slightly.

FLY LINES

Though the fly rod initiates the cast, it is the fly line that actually delivers the fly to its target. This differs from both spin and bait cast fishing, in which the weight of the lure pulls the line off the reel to its eventual target.

Early fly lines were woven from horsehair, later to be replaced by woven silk. Silk lines were beautiful to cast but were rather troublesome and inconvenient. Each night the fisherman had to remove the line from the reel for drying. The following morning he would then stretch and dress the line with an oil paste so that it would float. The remains of old line-drying racks are still found around many old fishing camps and lodges.

The 1950s saw silk replaced by synthetic fly lines, which completely revolutionized the fly fishing industry. Modern lines consist of a polyvinyl chloride material applied to a thin synthetic core. They are impervious to the rot that silk invited and require little maintenance. Since those designed to float do so naturally, a dressing is applied only to clean the line, rather than to add buoyancy. Dirt can cause a line to sink and will inhibit smooth casting.

FLY LINE MEASUREMENT

By design and function, all fly rods have a certain action, or flex. Some are very stiff and powerful. Others are soft and flexible. The proper fly line is one that balances or works within the flex of your rod. If the line is too heavy or too light the rod will not function optimally. Fortunately, fly lines come in different weights to meet standards dictated by different rods.

Silk lines were measured in diameter, with an obvious weight relationship. As the diameter got bigger so did the weight. Each diameter was assigned a letter, the largest being "A" and progressing to the smallest, "I," in 0.005-inch increments. If an angler bought a double-tapered silk line, he chose that combination of diameters that fit his rod flex. For example, "HCH" might appear as the line size, indicating that the line started at 0.025 inches (H), widened to a diameter of .050 (C) and then tapered back to .025 (H). To the novice angler this classification method was confusing at best.

Because of the synthetic material used, modern fly line is no longer measured in diameter but in grain weight. The first 30 feet of line is weighed and the line is then assigned a number from 2 (the lighest line) through 13 (the heaviest). The system is standardized throughout the fly line industry, and rod manufacturers helpfully indicate the correct line sizes to be used for any rod.

FLY LINE TAPERS

Fly lines come in a variety of tapers designed to facilitate casting and presentation of the fly. As a line is cast, the energy that initiated the cast diminishes, for there is no such thing as perpetual motion. To provide less resistance at the end of a cast as this energy dissipates, fly lines are tapered. There are several configurations.

Double Tapers

Starting at one end, the line gradually widens for approximately 20 feet, maintains the widened diameter for 50 feet, then gradually narrows to its original diameter over the final 20 feet.

Double taper is the most popular type of fly line and can be used for most kinds of trout fishing. It is easy to operate, presents the fly delicately, and its nicest feature is revealed when one end of the line becomes cracked and broken: It can be reversed.

Weight Forward

A weight forward fly line was designed for long casts, windy conditions, or big (fast-flowing) water. Today, weight forward is used in all types of fishing. In fact it has become almost as popular as double taper, and I recommend it to beginners and those seeking the greatest fly line versatility. In principle, the bulk of the line weight is at one end, and it is this weight that actually carries or "shoots" the line out. The weighted front portion is approximately 30 feet, and because it is tapered somewhat, the line works well for normal fishing distances.

Bass Bug/Saltwater Taper

Bass bug and saltwater taper is essentially a weight-forward fly line with a shorter, bulkier front taper, which helps to turn over the large, wind-resistant flies that bass and saltwater fishing often require.

Shooting Head

A shooting head is designed for extremely long casts. Basically, it is a tapered 30-foot line (versus the normal 90 feet) spliced to a special running line of monofilament or small-diameter fly line. Because of this small, slick-running line, which is attached to the reel, a shooting head can obtain a cast of 120 ft

Fly Line Configurations

Weight forward.
Specially designed weight forward line with long slender front taper for delicate presentation of small flies. Weight distribution of body section allows extra distance when required.

Bug taper.
Weight forward line with short front taper to "turn over" heavier, wind resistant cork and hair body bugs. The most practical choice for bass popping bugs.

Double taper.
Traditional line for handling trout flies, streamers and small popping bugs with finesse. Identical tapers on both ends—can be reversed as an economy measure. Perfect for roll casting.

Shooting taper.
For specialized long distance casting. 30 foot head with factory installed loop for easy attachment of monofilament or floating running line.

Level line.
For live bait fishing and when delicate fly presentation or long casts are not essential. An economy line.

or more. Monofilament as a running line can create problems, however. Its lightness and limpness make its drift difficult to control, which in turn limits control of the fly. If you're going to use a shooting head, (and I don't recommend it to beginners), stick to a small diameter fly line as the running line.

FLY LINE DENSITIES

Regardless of what line weight or taper you choose, fly lines come in different densities, from floating types for most fishing situations, to sinking types for subsurface fishing. A floating fly line is the most versatile and is used for perhaps 80 percent of fishing applications, and therefore it is the first type of line you should acquire. Sinking lines come in four densities: slow sinking, fast sinking, high density, and super high density. Today, even lead core lines are available. Miserable to cast, they do reach the bottom quickly.

There are also special purpose nymph lines, called sink tips and wetheads. The sink tip lines allow the first 10, 20, and 30 feet of line to sink while the rest floats. This feature lets you both control and mend the line, facilitating easier pick-up of the line off the water for recast. For deeper water situations "wetheads" or 30-foot sink tips are indicated: the first 30 feet sink and the remainder floats. The sinking portions of both wetheads and sink tips come in different sink rates.

READING FLY LINE DESIGNATIONS

DT6F, WF6F, WF6S, WF6F/S
The above fly line descriptions, appearing on boxes containing line, would be read from left to right, as follows: Double Taper size 6 Floating; Weight Forward size 6 Floating; Weight Forward size 6 Sinking; Weight Forward size 6 Float/Sink (or sink tip). The labeling on sinking type lines will also tell you the sink rate.

FLY LINE BACKING

Fly lines are usually 90 feet in length, and because a large fish can easily run out this amount of line it is imperative that we first place on the reel a braided Dacron line, called backing, which attaches to the fly line itself. Besides providing more overall line length, backing takes up space on the reel spool, allowing the fly line to be reeled in more quickly and stored on the spool in larger loops. Never use monofilament as a backing material since its tendency to stretch can cause reel-spool damage. How much backing you use depends on the size of the reel, the length and taper of line you are using, and the type of fishing you are doing. For most trout fishing, 50 to 100 yards of backing is adequate, while saltwater fishing requires 250 to 300 yards.

FLY LEADERS

Years ago, fly leaders were made of silkworm gut drawn from the internal silk sac of the Spanish silkworm. When dry, gut was brittle and would not stretch out its coiled memory. Fishermen could maintain the leaders' pliancy only by keeping the leaders dampened in a metal container.

Today's leaders are made of combinations of extruded nylons and polymers, providing far greater tensile strength than gut was ever capable of. Like fly lines, leaders are tapered to ease their casting. A heavy *butt* section attached to the fly line tapers through a mid-section called the *body*, and finally to an 18- to 24-inch section, called the *tippet*, at the end of which the fly is attached. Leaders are measured by the diameters of their tippets, and as you might guess, there is a close correlation between a tippet's diameter and its tensile strength. Larger diameter tippets are less susceptible to breakage, while smaller diameter tippets are less visible and less an encumbrance to the fly, making them the better choice against selective fish in clear, smooth waters. There are nine standard diameters, each classified with an X-code according to its size. Regardless of manufacturer, 8X represents a leader with a tippet diameter of .003 inches; 7X, one of .004 inches and so on, through 0X (8.5) inches to X4 (.015) inches. European leaders have the same X-classification, but diameters are measured in millimeters rather than inches.

Most leaders come pre-tapered or knotless from the manufacturer, although you can buy leader kits and tie your own compound leaders. Manufactured leaders usually come in seven-and-a-half-, nine-, and 12-foot lengths. Seven-and-a-half foot leaders are easiest for the novice to operate; they are also good for dry fly, wet fly, and nymph fishing in tight conditions. Nine-foot leader is the standard for most types of fishing, and 12-foot leaders are used for smooth, clear waters such as spring creeks, where distance between the fly line and the fly is critical. For super-delicate water a 16-foot leader can be used, although for many anglers it is difficult to cast and turn over. Very short leaders of six feet or less are often used for sink tip or full sinking fly line, enabling the leader to sink quickly and more uniformly (more on these terms in the next chapter).

LEADER TIPPET AND CORRESPONDING FLY SIZE

Leader Tip or Tippet		X Code	Pound Test	Fly-Hook Sizes
(Diameter in thousandths of an inch)	.003	8X	1.2	24,26,28,32
	.004	7X	2	20,22,24,26
	.005	6X	3	16,18,20,22
	.006	5X	4	14,16,18
	.007	4X	5	12,14,16
	.008	3X	6	10,12,14
	.009	2X	7	6,8,10
	.010	1X	8.5	2,4,6
	.011	0X	10	1/0,2,4
	.012	X1	12	2/0,1/0,2
	.013	X2	14	3/0,2/0,1/0,2
	.014	X3	16	5/0,4/0,3/0,2/0
	.015	X4	18	6/0,5/0,4/0,3/0

KNOTS

Over the years, I have become convinced that I am hired as a guide not to teach fly fishing, but to tie knots for people who have never taken the time to learn how. The easiest way to learn is to sit down and do them. Cocktail hour—if one doesn't imbibe too much—tends to be an especially convenient time to pick up a few pieces of monofilament and put in that essential practice time. The following are the basic knots that all fly fishermen should know:

The Nail Knot

The nail knot is for attaching fly line to backing, and leader to fly line. To tie it, lay the leader parallel with the fly line and a narrow finishing nail, being sure to leave enough of the leader hanging free. Now wrap this short end of the leader five times around the fly line, nail, and leader material itself. Next, run the end back up through the middle of all the lines, remove the nail, and tighten the knot. If you've wound the leader correctly, and not let the windings overlap, you should have a nice small knot. Snip away its ends and coat the knot with either contact cement or—my preference—clear nail polish. Nail knots create a smooth transition between line surfaces.

The nail knot.

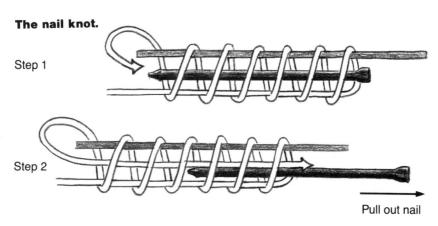

Step 1

Step 2

Pull out nail

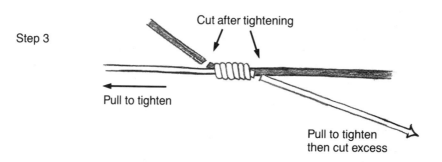

Step 3

Cut after tightening

Pull to tighten

Pull to tighten
then cut excess

The Blood Knot or Barrel Knot

The blood knot or barrel knot is designed to attach two pieces of monofilament together and is especially useful in attaching additional tippets to leader body. Since tapered leaders have only so much tippet material on them, in lieu of replacing the entire leader, you can attach an additional length of the desired-size tippet to the leader itself, using spools of tippet material, available at most fly fishing dealers. To make this attachment, the blood knot is one of the knots of choice.

Cross two pieces of monofilament. Wrap one end five turns down the long side of the other piece of mono. Bring the piece over and place it in the crotch or middle of the knot. Repeat the process with the other end of mono, bringing it back up through the hole, or crotch, formed by the other piece. Five turns with either end guarantees optimum holding strength and knot-seating. Now, wet the knot with your mouth and, holding the long lengths, slowly pull the knot tight. Clip the short ends to the base of the knot, and your blood knot is complete.

The blood knot, or barrel knot.

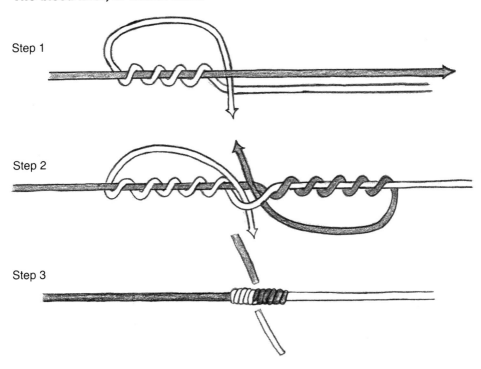

Step 1

Step 2

Step 3

Surgeon's Knot

The surgeon's knot also attaches two pieces of monofilament, and because of its ease, it is now preferred by many anglers to the blood knot. Essentially, it is a double overhand knot in which both pieces of monofilament are brought through the tying loop twice instead of once. It can be tied quickly and is very, very strong. Again, wet before tightening.

The surgeon's knot.

Step 1

Step 2

Step 3

Step 4

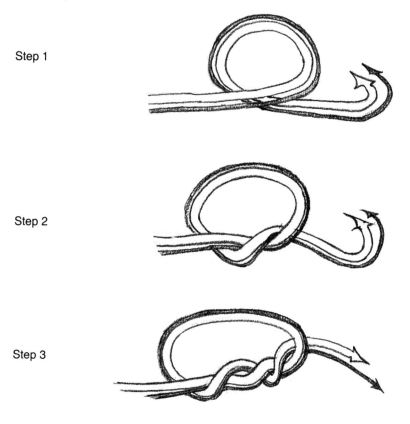

Clinch and Improved Clinch Knot

The clinch knot—also known as the cinch knot—is for fastening the leader to the fly. To start the clinch knot, thread the leader either up through or down through the eye of the hook. Wrap the end of the leader at least five times down its main length, and come back up through the gap between the eye and the wraps. Holding the fly and the main length of leader, moisten the knot and tighten. For an "improved" clinch knot, after you have gone through the gap between the eye and the wraps, continue to bring the short leader piece through the formed main loop. The key in tightening either knot is to pull on the main leader—*do not pull* on the small portion of leader, for the knot will not seat tightly against the hook.

The clinch knot.

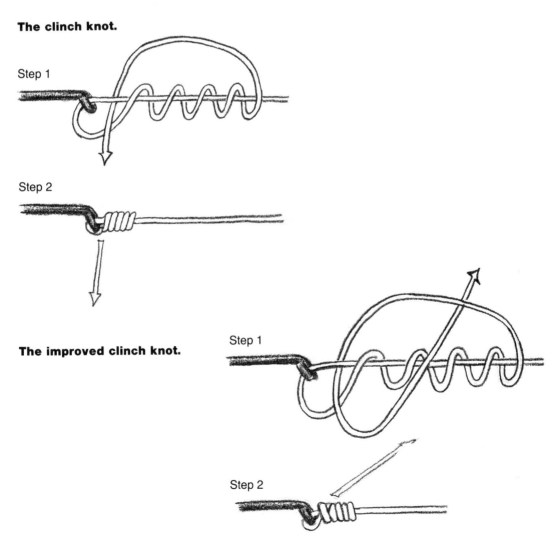

Step 1

Step 2

The improved clinch knot.

Step 1

Step 2

REEL SETUP

You now know something about rods, reels, lines, leaders, and backing. The methods for attaching backing to reel spool, fly line to backing, leader to fly line are as follows: 1) *To attach backing to the reel:* Thread line around the spool, and make an overhand knot around the reel spindle and another overhand knot at the end of the short piece (see diagram). Pull tightly and the knot should set against the spool with no slippage. After winding on backing, 2)

Reel-line setup.

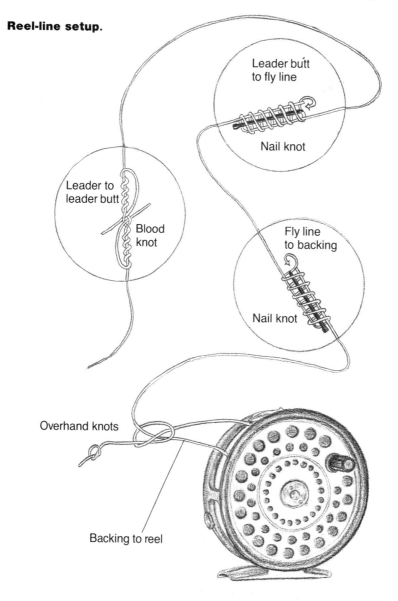

Leader butt
to fly line

Nail knot

Leader to
leader butt

Blood
knot

Fly line
to backing

Nail knot

Overhand knots

Backing to reel

attach the fly line to the backing with a nail knot, then wind it on.

3) After the fly line is on reel, many fishermen tie on a heavy, 12-inch piece of 0.023″ monofilament known as a *butt section.* This is done for easier attachment of the leader and to prevent continual cutting back of the fly line. Again, the nail knot is used to attach the monofilament to the fly line. A tapered leader is then attached to the butt by means of a blood or surgeon's knot (4).

STRINGING UP THE ROD

Now that you have placed the appropriate backing, fly line, and leader on the reel, and have mounted it on the rod, it's time to string the rod for actual fishing. There is no real wrong way to accomplish this final task, but there is a generally accepted method to eliminate aggravation. In threading the line through the rod guides, double over the fly line itself instead of using the leader tippet, which is often difficult to see and manipulate. A doubled over fly line is easier to see and handle and will not slide back though the guides if the line slips from your fingers.

Now that your fly rod is strung and ready to go, you're ready to learn how to fly cast.

The Loop Trick

Doubling the line (A) makes threading it through the rod's guides easy (B). In addition, the line can't slip back.

A

B

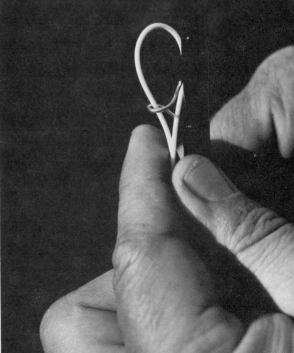

3

Fly Casting

Casting is an important component of fly fishing, but as you will learn while progressing through the sport, it is not the most important. That statement may come as a surprise, but in fact, the selection of a fly, where the fly is placed, how the fly operates while on or in the water—all these things take precedence over the casting operation. Fly casting is often overemphasized to the point of intimidating the beginning angler. Casting myths are numerous and often perpetuated by those fishermen who themselves have not mastered all aspects of the sport.

For many years, if you could cast a fly you were thought to be an expert. Little attention was paid to whether you caught any fish; that was more or less assumed. Each year I watch fly fishermen, dressed to the nines, casting a beautiful line with few results. What fish these "around the bend fishermen" manage to catch are mysteriously taken in places too remote and rugged for others to document.

To put it plainly, *the correlation between catching fish and your ability to cast a line is minimal.* Many practitioners will tell a novice that fly casting is just too hard to learn. Nonsense! Practice will make you a better caster, but even without practice, most people, in a very short time, can learn to cast a fly well enough to catch fish.

Another myth believed by many beginners is that you must cast great distances before you're able to catch fish. In fact, most fish taken on a fly are hooked anywhere from ten to 25 feet from the angler, not the 80 or 100 feet that some anglers would have you believe. Every year, without fail, I have fishermen tell me how they made a 90-foot cast, dropping a dry fly within a circle the size of a teacup and taking the 20-inch trout that was quietly sipping naturals (that is, natural insects) off the surface. To make the story more

49

Solid, efficient fly casting is merely a means to an end—catching fish.

interesting, the storyteller will sometimes throw in a 20-mile-per-hour cross-wind. In actuality, even if your hand-eye coordination was exceptional, the vast amount of slack line on the water would make setting the hook extremely difficult at that distance. No, sorry: If a fish *is* caught at 90 feet, more than likely the fish was responsible for the accident, not the long-distance caster.

Anglers, even professional instructors, all have their egos and would like you to believe there is only one way to cast—*their* way. Such is not the case. Granted, there are certain points and functions that should be learned and adhered to, but because people have different physiques and abilities, everyone will develop his own casting style. The same point applies to any sport. For example, all professional golfers have slightly different swings from each other, but all, when they hit the ball, apply the same basic principles. Adapting our unique characteristics to basic principles is the key to successful fly casting just as it is to successful golf.

PRINCIPLES OF THE CAST

The function of fly casting is to get the fly from point A to point B as efficiently as possible. It is only a means to an end and should be looked upon as just that. Our intent is to catch fish, not to impress them or other people with the beauty of the cast. And don't think for a second that a fish is going to say, "That was a beautiful tight loop, Mr. Jones; therefore, I will take your fly."

Fly casting requires little or no strength. It is the *flexing* and *reflexing,* often referred to as the *loading* and *unloading* of the rod, that makes the line work. Because strength is not a requirement for successful casting, many women and children often acquire the techniques more readily than beginning males, since they don't try to muscle (or "macho") the rod. They let the rod do the work, systematically using the hands, wrist, and arm to set the flexing and reflexing action of the rod in motion.

Fly rod function is analogous to pole-vaulting. The vaulter plants the pole, and his own body weight (plus momentum) loads the vaulting pole with energy. However, it is not his strength that lifts him up and over the bar. No, it is the release of that energy along the flexible shaft that drives him up and over. The same thing happens with a fly rod: The weight of the line loads the rod, and the movement of the arm and the flick of the wrist set the rod in motion, delivering the line.

The basic fly cast consists of a *backcast* and a *forward cast.* The parameters of these motions have traditionally been taught as related to the hand positions

Casting: Rod Position

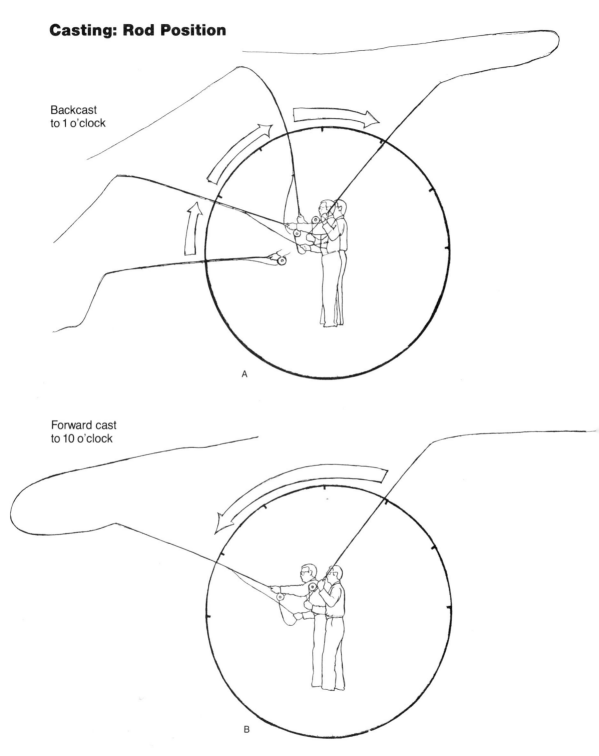

Backcast
to 1 o'clock

Forward cast
to 10 o'clock

A

B

The backcast starts with the rod at the nine o'clock position, ending at one o'clock (A). The forward cast starts at the one o'clock position, ending at ten o'clock (B).

on a clock, and this is still a good way of thinking about it. The backcast is started with the rod in the nine o'clock position, ending at one o'clock. The forward cast starts at one o'clock and ends at ten o'clock.

It is important to think of the cast in these terms, for the beginning caster needs to know what position his rod should be in throughout the cast.

Before you begin to practice your fly casting, choose a place without obstructions such as trees, shrubs, fences, or buildings. Obviously, a pond would be ideal, but a lawn, a swimming pool, or an actual river will work as well. Avoid a practice location that is on dirt or concrete pavement, for damage to the fly line can occur. I also recommend not using an actual fly with a hook, for it can become an eye-injuring weapon, certainly in the hands of a beginner. All that is needed to simulate a fly is a small piece of yarn, of the approximate weight of a fly, tied to the end of a leader. This will aid not only in turning over the leader when cast, but also in your developing some degree of accuracy.

The Backcast

To start, pick up the rod and grip it with the thumb extended on top of the handle. If this feels uncomfortable, a simple baseball grip can also be used. There are some who extend their index finger down the rod grip, but I have found that after a day of casting or of handling very big rods, the index finger and hand will get fatigued. To avoid this, get in the habit of extending the thumb.

Before you start the backcast, strip off from the reel and extend through the guides approximately 20 feet of fly line. If you are right-handed, hold the line in your left hand tightly but comfortably, at about waist level. When first learning to fly cast, don't get in the habit, although many do it, of gripping the fly line itself in the rod hand, for this position is improper in actual fishing and casting situations. Holding the line in the opposite hand is also more efficient; you can add more line to the cast simply by loosening the grip of the line itself in your hand.

The term "backcast" is to some extent misleading. It implies that the beginning portion of the cast goes directly back. In reality, you not only go back, but you actually lift the rod as well. Consequently, I call this portion of the cast the "up and back cast."

With ten to 15 feet of line extending from the rod tip, place the rod in the nine o'clock position. As you slowly raise the rod, reaching the ten o'clock position, the weight and tension of the line will cause the rod to load, or flex. Upon reaching ten o'clock apply the "power stroke" (a term I use lightly) or quick wrist flick, which will activate the rod tip and start the line up and behind

Gripping the Fly Rod

Correct grip.   The baseball grip (also correct).   A not-recommended grip.

you. This stroke is stopped at about 12 o'clock, at which point you lock your wrist and, while the line uncoils behind you, drift your arm and rod to the one o'clock position. With the rod in the one o'clock position, you have reached the most critical point for a begining caster, because it is here that the most common mistake is made: the tendency of the beginner to break his wrist, going beyond the one o'clock position. Some experienced anglers can get away with a wrist break, but for a novice it means trouble, allowing the line to hit the ground and/or not letting the line extend above and behind you.

To avoid breaking the wrist past one o'clock, novice fly casters were once taught to keep the arm close to the body. In fact, it was recommended that something breakable and valuable, but thin—like a full pint of whisky—be held under the armpit while the cast was in motion to properly motivate the learner. Today, however, we teach that the arm is a mere extension of the rod, which gives casting a more fluid arm movement. If you have trouble finding one o'clock with the rod, try 12; if that doesn't work, try 11. Slowly you will find the right spot at which to stop your arm movement.

The Backcast

(Note: All rod positions in the photographs are the mirror image of clock positions mentioned in the captions. Thus, when the rod is at three o'clock in the photograph, think nine o'clock; when the rod is at eleven o'clock, think one o'clock, etc.)

Before the backcast begins, the rod should be at the nine o'clock position, with 20 feet of line extended (A).

To begin the backcast, lift the rod to the ten o'clock position (B). This causes the road to begin flexing, or "loading."

As the line travels backward, let the arm and rod drift back approximately to the one o'clock position (E).

When the rod reaches the one o'clock position, the wrist should be *locked*. At all costs, avoid breaking the wrist beyond this position (F).

Upon reaching the ten o'clock position, apply the power stroke by quickly flicking the wrist and stopping at 11:30 (C). Note how the rod attains a fully loaded position.

After you halt the power stroke, the rod quickly unloads or reflexes (D). This causes the line to be driven backwards. Remember: It is the rod's loading and unloading action that makes the cast work, *not* the strength of the caster.

At the end of the backcast, the line should be fully extended behind you (G).

**Good rod position at
the end of the backcast.**

At one o'clock, hesitate slightly, allowing the line to completely lay out behind you. When the line reaches its full extension and before it begins to drop down below the plane of the rod tip, you should begin the forward cast. Don't wait too long, for letting the line drop too low causes additional problems. When to start the forward movement of the rod is a matter of timing and feel. A good way to learn this important maneuver is to turn slightly around and look for the fully extended line. Once you learn the proper timing, however, you should stop "peeking" and rely on your feel of the rod either tugging or reloading. A tug at one o'clock means the weight of the line is reflexing or reloading the rod, preparing it for the forward cast.

The Forward Cast

The most common mistake the inexperienced caster makes on starting the forward cast is flicking the wrist from one o'clock in an effort to get the line forward. Don't do it. Instead, start the forward movement by driving or pushing the rod forward while maintaining the rod in the one o'clock position. Some people call this first forward cast movement the "punch." The rod has not moved from the one o'clock position—it has only been driven from the shoulder to a point out in front of us. What this very important movement does is load and flex the rod and help straighten out the line behind you.

The Forward Cast

At the instant the line is fully extended behind you, begin the forward cast. You do this *not* by flicking the wrist forward, but by driving, or punching, the rod forward (A). This driving or punching action further straightens the line and starts the rod-loading process for the forward cast.

With the rod fully loaded (flexed) and in front of you, flick your wrist forward quickly to send the line on its forward flight (B).

After flicking the wrist forward, stop the rod at the ten o'clock position (C). Again, it is the unloading of the flexed rod that makes the cast work, not the strength of the caster. *(continued on next page)*

The Forward Cast (Cont.)

As the line begins to travel forward, the rod should remain at ten o'clock (D).

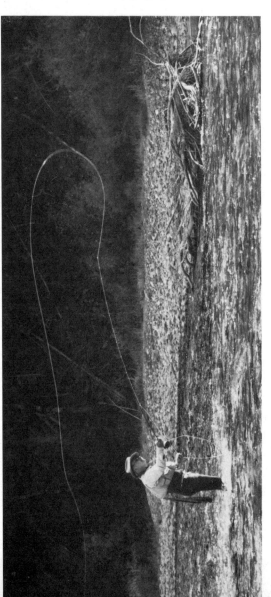

For line control and accuracy, the loop of the fly line should be tight and even (E). Loop tightness is determined by how quickly you flick your wrist. A slow flick opens the line, creating a wider loop.

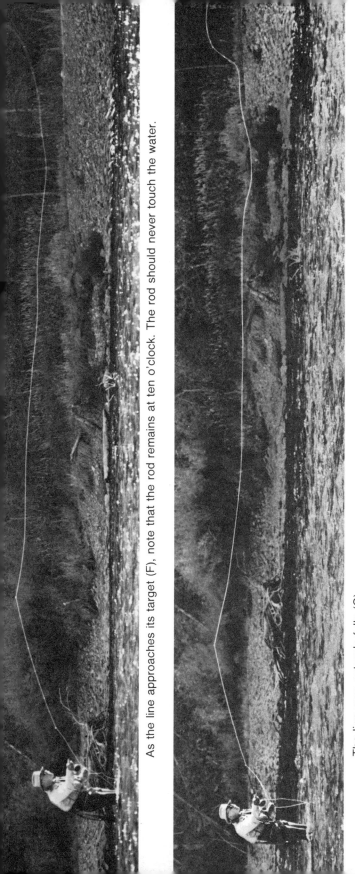

As the line approaches its target (F), note that the rod remains at ten o'clock. The rod should never touch the water.

The line now extends fully (G) . . .

. . . and falls to the water's surface (H). Note that the rod remains at the ten o'clock position.

The Forward Drive, or Punch

The drive, or punch, is perhaps the most important part of the forward cast. With the rod at one o'clock (A), do not flick the wrist, but first punch, or drive, the arm forward (B), until the rod is slightly in front of you. Then, and only then, do you flick your wrist forward (C), initiating the forward cast.

Once the rod and hand are slightly in front of you, flick your wrist, which unloads (unflexes) the rod, causing the line to be driven forward. Stop the arm and wrist flick at ten o'clock, allowing the line to fully extend and drop to the water as a complete unit. Do not bring the rod to nine o'clock, or the line will hit the water with a disturbing splash.

As you drive the rod forward on the forward cast, it is important to drive for a point on the horizon. Do not drive upward for the sky, nor downward for the water. If the line's horizontal plane is thrown at too vertical an angle, the line, when extended, will pile back on the water, on top of itself. Guides call this mistake a bull's-eye cast, the line making rings around itself and the fly falling in the middle. The line should fully extend out, then drop as a unit, and of its own accord, to the water.

Tight Loops

As the line moves backward on the backcast and, most important, forward on the forward cast, your objective is to achieve a tight loop with the line. Tight loops give greater accuracy and also slice through high winds with greater efficiency. Tight loops are directly related to how quickly—not powerfully—you flick your wrist to actuate the rod tip (literally, to put it into mechanical motion). If on the forward cast you turn the wrist over slowly, the rod tip will unflex slowly, causing the line to roll out in a wide loop. If the wrist is turned over quickly, the rod tip actuates quickly, providing the desired tight loop.

SOLVING CASTING PROBLEMS

It is important to note that fly casting, like any other mechanical sport, requires practice. Casting efficiency does not come automatically and does require a certain amount of work. But regardless of your casting abilities, there are certain mistakes and problems that do develop time and again to casters at all levels. The following is a list of the most common casting problems encountered.

Backcasts Not Reaching Full Extension

If your backcast does not extend the line fully, undoubtedly you are not applying enough power, or snap, on the backcast motion to drive the line back. Remember, the rod is not a fairy wand; you can't baby it and you must use some authority. Apply more power and snap when lifting the line off the water.

Snapping the Line on Forward Cast

Snapping the line is caused by not allowing the line to extend fully outwards on the backcast. Still uncoiling when the forward cast is started, the line snaps, or pops, like a bullwhip. To avoid line snapping, allow the line to extend completely by hesitating a bit longer before starting the forward cast.

Catching the Ground Behind You

Catching ground and bushes behind you is a common problem for the beginner. The cause is either waiting too long at the end of the backcast, allowing the line to fall, or, as in most cases, allowing the rod to travel past the one o'clock position, a consequence of breaking your wrist.

To correct the first problem, shorten your delay in starting the forward cast. If you are breaking your wrist—*the most common mistake*—you should pay attention to where your rod is positioned at the end of the backcast. If visualizing the rod at one o'clock is difficult, try thinking of the rod position at 12 o'clock, or perpendicular to the ground.

Breaking the Wrist When Casting

Breaking the wrist, or allowing the rod to go far beyond the one o'clock position, is the beginning caster's single most common mistake.

The Consequences of Breaking the Wrist

A

B

Breaking the wrist on the backcast initiates a host of problems. First, the line fails to extend fully, instead hitting the water behind you (A). Second, the line is not straight for the forward cast (B), resulting in a cast that does not drive out smartly in a tight loop (C), but rather, dies and falls to the water in a heap (D).

C

D

Line Piles Upon Water on Forward Cast

When the line has been driven toward the sky rather than toward the horizon, the line piles up on itself. Your angle of attack is wrong. Also, when starting your forward cast, you're probably flicking your wrist immediately, rather than driving or punching the rod forward before snapping the wrist. Again, the line should be driven to a position *on the horizon* and allowed to drop to the water as a unit.

Wide Uncontrollable Loops

When the loops of your forward cast become very wide, or open, accuracy eludes you. The cause of wide loops lies in the quickness with which the wrist is snapped on the forward cast. To rectify the problem and create tight loops, simply snap the wrist quicker; don't roll the wrist.

Fly Catches or Hooks on Line at End of Forward Cast

Hooking your fly on the line on the forward cast is a very common problem. Overpowering the rod—applying more strength and power than the rod flex can handle—is the most common cause. The result is a delayed reaction. To fix this, ease up on your power stroke. Also, chances are you have not driven or punched the rod forward from the one o'clock position. Driving—punching forward—is a must if the rod and line are to work well together.

The Line Splashes the Water

Line splash disturbs fish, which never helps the fisherman. In most cases, you have not stopped the rod at ten o'clock during the forward cast, allowing the line to fall of its own accord. The rod tip touches the water, causing the line to crash upon the surface. To correct this, halt the forward cast at ten o'clock, allowing the line to extend fully and fall gently as a unit to the water.

Unconsciously Casting Sidearm

The beginning caster should learn to cast in a straight up-and-down motion, not sidearm. Greater accuracy of fly presentation will result. There will be occasions, because of low-hanging shrubbery, when a side cast is necessary, but still the basic components of the cast remain the same. The clock face is still the reference point: The cast begins at nine, stops at one and comes back to ten—all we have done is laid the clock on its side.

OTHER IMPORTANT FLY CASTS

The Roll Cast

The roll cast is very useful and practical for all anglers of all abilities. It has many applications but is most often used when an angler has a large obstruction directly behind him, making a normal backcast impossible. The roll cast is easy to do, so much so that some of my beginning students have asked why they can't use the roll cast instead of the normal cast.

To start, lay 15 or 20 feet of fly line on the water. It is best to try the roll cast on water, as water creates sufficient tension for the line to operate efficiently. Slowly raise the rod until it reaches the one o'clock position and then *stop.* Remember, you can't make a backcast. The line should now be to the *outside* of the rod and a portion of the line should also be lying on the water. After line and rod have come to a complete stop, drive the rod forward and flick the wrist. The line will roll up and out.

The basic roll cast has multiple uses. The roll cast pickup, for example, is used to take the fly off the water and start the normal cast. After making a normal roll cast without letting the fly and line hit the water on the forward roll, start the backcast when the fly and line are in the air.

You can also change direction with the roll cast. Because streams have current, the fly will eventually end up below you. To get the fly and line upstream or into a more favorable casting position, roll the rod in the direction you wish to go and you will find that the line will follow the rod. This can be done either to the right or to the left. Remember, the basic roll cast technique still applies.

The Roll Cast

To start the roll cast, allow 15 to 20 feet of line to lay in front of you (A).

Slowly lift the rod to the one o'clock position, allowing the fly line to hang both behind and to the outside of the rod. When the rod reaches the one o'clock position, bring it to a complete but momentary stop (B).

With the rod driven forward, the line begins its rollout (E),

To start the forward cast, first drive, or punch the rod forward, hard, then flick the wrist. This starts the line forward (C).

The line on the water creates both tension and resistance, causing the rod to flex and load. Remember, the rod does the work. Your arm and wrist merely set it in motion (D).

sending the fly to its target (F).

The Wind Cast

Wind is the fly fisherman's nemesis. I know people who literally reel up their lines and hang up their rods when wind appears. Unfortunately, they are missing some good angling opportunities—fish don't stop feeding (unless a hatch is blown off) just because the wind blows.

Wind blowing directly in your face, although not pleasant, can be dealt with by increasing line speed through the use of the double-haul cast (more in a moment). Crosswinds create greater problems. If you are a right-handed caster and the wind is blowing left to right, the line and the fly will be blown away from you, diminishing your cast's accuracy. When the wind is blowing

The Wind Cast

Crosswinds are never fun, especially those that blow the fly and line against you. To avoid this problem, move the cast to the opposite side of your body, where the fly will be blown away from you (A).

Using the basic casting motion, lift the rod at an angle over your head (B), not across your body.

Backcast, following the basic clock positions (although now the clockface is parallel to the water) (C).

right to left, the situation worsens; to some right-handed casters, the fly can quickly become a lethal weapon. To rectify this problem, simply move the cast from the right side of the body over to the left. Remember, you are still making your normal cast. The motion stays within the confines of the clock, but instead of taking the rod straight up and down, lift the rod at an angle up *over your head,* until the rod tip is on your left side. Go through the normal motions of a cast; the line and fly will be blown away from you instead of into your body. Do not make the cast with your arm coming across the chest, as the motion is awkward and generates little power. In any wind situation, it pays to keep your casting loops tight.

Let the line extend fully be-hind you on the backcast (D). Then . . .

Drive, or punch the rod forward to start the forward cast (E).

The line will drive out, just as with a regular cast, with no loss of power or accu-racy (F).

The Reach Cast

Most river systems have multiple currents. Between you and your target area there will inevitably be a fast section of water that, when the line lands, will drag the fly out of position. One way to alleviate this problem is to use what is known as a *reach cast,* which throws the line upstream or, if necessary, downstream, depending on the current.

To complete the reach cast, make your normal cast, but when starting the forward movement, as the line begins to uncoil in front of you, and before the line lays out completely, quickly throw or reach out to the side with the rod in the direction you wish to go. That will put the line upstream or downstream of the selected holding water. The reach cast is easy to perform and can resolve many of the fly's float and drift problems.

The Reach Cast to the Right

The reach cast, which can be made to the left or right, has many uses, but is generally used to offset multiple current problems. To reach cast to the right, start your normal forward cast (A).

As the line shoots forward, and while it is still above the water, extend both the rod and your arm to the right (B).

With the rod in this position, let the line fall to the water (C).

The Reach Cast to the Left

To perform a reach cast to the left, once again start with the basic casting motion (A).

As the line begins to lay out, extend your arm and rod either across your body or over your head, again while the line is in the air (B).

Let the line fall to the water (C).

The Double Haul

The double haul should not be undertaken until you've mastered the basic cast, but once you have reached an intermediate level, you should include the double haul in your repertoire of casts. The double haul is used, 1) for achieving greater distance and, 2) when irritating wind becomes a problem. Essentially, with the double haul you are increasing the line speed to roughly half again what it would be with a normal cast.

Performing the double haul is a bit like rubbing your stomach and patting your head at the same time. It requires two simultaneous movements, both on the backcast and on the forward cast. The cast is initiated with the rod in the normal starting position. With your opposite hand holding the fly line halfway between the reel and the first stripping guide, lift the rod in a normal casting

A   B

The Double Haul

The double haul is used for attaining greater casting distance and cutting through wind. Both are achieved by increasing the speed of the line on the forward cast. As you start your backcast, simultaneously pull down on the line held in the opposite hand (A, B).

motion, and at the same time, pull down sharply on the fly line with your opposite hand. As the line extends on the backcast, let your rod arm, along with the opposite hand holding the line, drift up and back to the one o'clock position. On the forward cast, as you drive the rod forward, again pull down sharply on the line with the opposite hand. As the rod reaches ten o'clock, release the line and let the remaining line shoot through the guides.

   In learning the double haul, it is best to take it in steps. First, perfect the backcast portion. After you've coordinated the line pull and the cast correctly, try the forward cast. After both have been mastered, put them together. You

C

As the line extends behind you, let both the line and your hand drift upward with the momentum of the back-cast (C).

D

As you start to drive, or punch, the forward cast, once again pull down on the line held in the opposite hand (D).

E

With the line out in front of you, you can either let any remaining line shoot through the guides to finish the cast (E), or repeat the double haul procedure.

will probably be amazed at your ability. Remember, don't overpower the rod. A natural casting stroke, quickness, and power are all that's needed.

The above casts should be learned by every caster. But remember, fly casting is only a means to an end. As you will learn, if the correct fly is not on the leader, and the fly is not correctly presented to the fish, the best casters in the world will never accomplish their goal. It's not necessary to look stylish or pretty while casting, as long as you become efficient. After you examine all aspects of the sport, I am sure you will agree that casting is what it is—just casting.

4

Trout and Their Senses

Fish possess certain important senses that all anglers should understand. In this chapter, we'll study the habits and characteristics of trout, for it is those fish that fly anglers most frequently pursue. In later chapters, we will concentrate on saltwater and warmwater species.

The trout is certainly the most common target of fly fishermen. It is synonymous with the sport. Therefore, as an angler you should learn to recognize the various trout species and understand their habits relative to their environment.

THE CUTTHROAT TROUT
(Salmo clarki)

Years ago, fish biologist and author Paul Needham, in his books *Trout Streams* and *A Guide to Freshwater Biology,* placed the cutthroat at the top of the trout hierarchy. He considered the cutthroat the true trout, from which evolved the rainbow and the golden. Today, many fish taxonomists—specialists in fish classification—question this theory, instead believing that some other (distant) ancestor is the forerunner of all trout, including the cutthroat.

The cutthroat was the original trout in the West. Its range covered the entire Rocky Mountains west to the Pacific Coast. Within that immense geographical area are found numerous subspecies, many of which are located only short distances from one another. Today all cutthroat are classified and referred to under the Latin name *Salmo clarki.*

From an identification standpoint, the cutthroat gets its name from the two red slashes that appear under and on the outside of its lower jaw. Its

75

An 18-inch rainbow trout uses sound, smell, and sight
to move in on its prey.

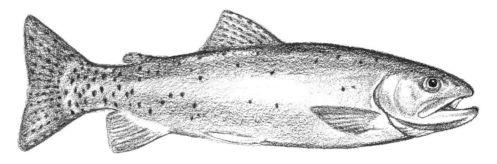

brownish yellow sides are highlighted by black spots, and some anglers refer to the fish as "the black spotted trout." Because the cutthroat is closely related to the rainbow, the two can and will spawn together, both in the wild and through hatchery programs. This unique cross produces what is called a "cutbow," a fish with a superb growth rate but little reproductive capacity, especially in hatchery-reared fish.

From a fisherman's standpoint, the true cutthroat, although not as active when hooked as a rainbow or a brown, is a great fish. Because pure cutthroat fisheries are likely to be in remote locations, the fish is somewhat easily deceived by the fly. On the Yellowstone River, cutthroat, although selective as the season progresses, for the most part can be disappointingly easy prey.

Since cutthroat migrate to the sea, they provide good sport for Northwest fishermen as they feed along the estuaries before entering the river systems to spawn.

The cutthroat is a very important species, one that needs our protection if it is to survive.

THE RAINBOW TROUT
(Salmo gairdneri)

If the trout family has a world traveler it would have to be the rainbow, for it has been introduced in countless trout streams in North and South America, Europe, New Zealand, and Australia. Only the brown trout rivals the rainbow in its range of distribution and transplantation.

Originally, the rainbow was found on Pacific coastal streams of the western United States. But because fish culturists and hatchery managers found the rainbow so easy to propagate, it quickly became *the* trout for transplant.

The first rainbow eggs were transported to Michigan in the 1870s, and thereafter the eggs were quickly introduced to the Eastern Seaboard streams. Most of that original stock came from the subspecies *Salmo shasta,* a native of the McCloud and Kern rivers in northern California. Referred to as either the McCloud or Kern River strain of rainbow, today's fish, because of overzealous fish culturalization, have unfortunately altered their genetic structure, making identification of the original stock difficult.

The rainbow, like the cutthroat, is highly migratory and has many subspecies throughout the United States and Mexico. Taxonomists once felt that the influence of salt water divided the family of rainbow into two distinct species, *gairdneri* (what was called steelhead) and its freshwater cousin *irideus* (the non-migratory strain). Today, regardless of these early distinctions, all rainbow trout are scientifically termed *Salmo gairdneri.*

The rainbow is easily distinguished by a red stripe that travels the length of the fish from gill plates to tail and by hundreds of black spots covering the dorsal (back) side of the body. For anglers, the rainbow has few equals. It can be highly selective and at the same time quite "gregarious" in coming to your offering. When hooked, it puts on a display of long runs and active aerials, for which it has become renowned. There is no doubt that the rainbow trout will always be central to the fly fisherman's world.

The rainbow trout.

THE BROWN TROUT
(Salmo trutta)

If there is one trout that quickly gains the respect of fly fishermen throughout the world, it has to be the brown trout. Not an American breed, the brown comes from a range that originally covered large parts of Europe and Asia. In all probability this was the "speckled fish" that the Macedonians were catching with their primitive flies in northern Greece 4,000 years ago.

The brown trout arrived on this continent in the early 1880s and immediately received criticism from the brook trout fishermen of the Eastern Seaboard. Because of its intelligence and determination to survive, the unsophisticated approaches that were adequate for catching brook trout failed with the brown. For this reason the brown trout has survived nicely in many eastern and midwestern trout streams over the years. Later, the brown was planted in the northern Rockies, South America, and New Zealand, ranking it a close second to the rainbow in world distribution.

Because it is more difficult to raise in hatcheries, the brown trout's use in stream planting programs has been limited. Fish culturists, however, have come to realize that because of its ability to withstand warmer temperatures, marine degradations, and fishing pressure, the brown may be the trout of the future.

A migratory fish, the brown, like the rainbow, was divided into sea-run and freshwater varieties. The sea-run fish was called *Salmo fario* and the stay-at-home fish *Salmo trutta,* which has now become the generic taxonomic name for the species as a whole. There is also a distinction made between the original strains. Those that came from Germany were referred to as the "German brown"; the others, reared in a Scottish hatchery, were known as the "Lochlaven brown." Today, the two are difficult, if not impossible, to distinguish and are known collectively as German brown.

The brown trout.

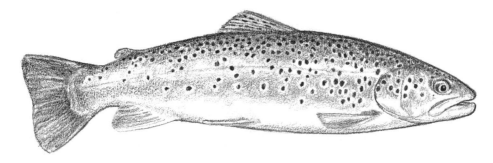

The brown trout is easily recognized by its butter-colored sides, high-lighted by black and red spots that follow the lateral line of its body. Early American fishermen thought it to be ugly compared to the beautiful brook trout, but today our fondness for the fish has rendered it a beautiful specimen indeed.

From a fishing standpoint, the brown has no peer. A cut above other trout in intelligence, it demands knowledge, experience, and cunning of the fisherman who tricks it into taking his fly. When hooked, it runs for every obstacle in the stream that might entangle your line. A true warrior, it will make long runs, jump, and totally exhaust itself in the effort to get free. Each time I catch a brown trout, regardless of its size, I have an inner feeling of accomplishment that I don't necessarily get from catching other trout. I am one of those who truly believe that the brown is a cut above its brothers.

THE BROOK TROUT
(Salvelinus fontinalis)

The brook trout was the original trout of the eastern and midwestern United States—the eastern counterpart of the cutthroat. From the north, in Canada, its range extended south to the streams of Georgia and west as far as the headwaters of the Mississippi. It was this beautiful fish at which early North American fishing was aimed.

Strictly speaking, the brook is not a trout, but belongs to the char family, which includes the Lake Trout, Dolly Varden, Arctic Char, and a few other species. Its scientific name is *Salvelinus fontinalis,* meaning "fish of the springs." Its char characteristics require that it live in very clear and cold water, and because of that requirement, populations have continually shrunk in the East and Midwest, where the above requirements have disappeared. Today the largest brook trout are found in the cold, remote reaches of its northern range and in the West where there is coldwater seepage.

Because the brook does not live as long as other trout species (usually four to six years compared to a rainbow's or brown's six to eight years), it never achieves immense size. The largest on record is only 14½ pounds, caught on the Nipigon River in Ontario, Canada, by Dr. W.J. Cook. Larger brook trout have been reported in South America, but none officially documented. Today, the largest brooks are caught in Labrador and Argentina.

Brook trout planted in western Rocky Mountain streams differ genetically from their eastern forebears due to hatchery techniques. Overpopulation from

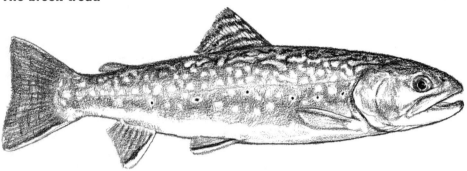

planting is the general rule, especially in high lakes and beaver ponds, and as a result, brook trout tend to run small.

The brook trout is probably the most beautiful of our freshwater fish. Its sides and back are various shades of gunmetal grey, highlighted by cream, orange, and red spots. Its fins are nicely edged in white, and during spawning the belly will turn a lovely orange-red color.

Fishermen prize brook trout not just for their good looks but also for their active defense of their freedom—and for their culinary qualities. A bit "gregarious" and many times a little foolish, they accept a fly readily and are easily caught. Fishermen who breakfast on their catch will always rank the brook at the top of the list. Since their populations are not hurt by the elimination of a few fish, the brook trout is ideal for a streamside meal.

THE GOLDEN TROUT
(Salmo aquabonita)

A high altitude fish, the golden trout is found in the streams and lakes of the California mountains and the Rockies. As a general rule you must hike to find them. Because of their habitat, goldens are smaller than rainbows and browns.

The golden, *Salmo aquabonita,* originated in the headwaters of the Kern River in California and was transported to other alpine locations in Idaho, Wyoming, Montana, and some other western states. Today the largest of the species, reaching 10¼ pounds, have been caught in these northern Rockies locations.

This trout is instantly recognized by its solid golden color, highlighted by a few black spots and red striping along its lateral line, belly, and gill plates.

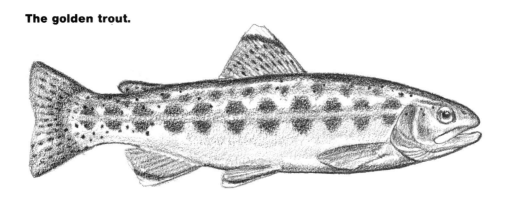

It rivals the brookie as one of the prettiest and most unusual-looking of the trout.

Because goldens live in high lakes they may exhibit a fickleness that is characteristic of alpine dwellers. Determining their specific aquatic diet will help, and when that is discovered and appropriately matched, they accept standard flies easily. When hooked, goldens can be as active as any other fish, depending on the temperature of the lake. To catch one of size is always a treat that more than justifies the long walk and difficult search for the golden's secret hiding spot.

TROUT PHYSIOLOGY AND SENSES

To fully understand trout behavior, and thus be able to fool them with a fly, you must know something about their sensory apparatus—hearing, smell, and sight. Thanks to their aquatic environment and the challenges to their survival, trout have evolved especially sophisticated sense organs.

Many anglers make the mistake of assuming trout and other fish to be stupid. Our experience with hatchery-raised, pen-fed fish has probably reinforced this attitude. But fish raised in the wild are far from stupid; in fact, they often prove to be brilliant when matched against a fisherman. This brilliance, of course, is not manifested in the form of reasoning, but rather in an acute, instinctive cunning.

Sound

Fish do hear, but in different and in some respects more sophisticated ways than humans do. They not only detect frequencies within the range of the human ear, but can also distinguish very low frequencies that are inaudible to us.

Fish have two sound receptors. The first runs along the lateral length of the fish's body and is designed to pick up general frequency vibrational information. The second receptor is an ear, located in the inner skull, used to detect the movement of tiny aquatic organisms, which make up the fish's diet. The ear can pick up frequencies very much lower than the human ear can detect and thus are able to locate invertebrates even when the water is murky. The sound of a large fly, such as a grasshopper, landing on the water is well within the range of this ear.

A fish cannot distinguish the human voice outside its water environment because the water acts as a muffler. Talking loudly on a trout stream therefore will not disturb the fish. On the other hand, throwing rocks into the water, banging oars on the sides of boats, or wading clumsily is easily identified as a danger signal by the fish.

Smell

The olfactory sensors in fish are much more sophisticated than once was thought. Years ago, it was not quite understood how salmon and other migratory fish found their way back to their original spawning beds. Credit for this amazing feat has now been assigned to the fish's olfactory system, and this is a clue to just how sensitive fish smelling apparatus in general is, especially when it comes upon alien odors. Because man comes from an environment with an array of smells that have nothing to do with the aquatic world, he can unsuspectingly transmit many alarming odors to the fish. The smell of tobacco and, worse, petroleum-based products such as insect repellant, line cleaners, and fly dressings can warn fish away from your fly.

Friends and I once gathered handfuls of live grasshoppers and offered them to the fish, producing a frenzy of enthusiastic feeding activity. Next, I presented a close artificial imitation dressed with a commercial silicone-based fly floatant. A fish quickly rose to the surface but would not take; it followed about an inch away, finally slipping back to its holding spot. We then applied to the same artificial fly a product designed both to float the fly and to disguise human odors; the same fish was quickly caught and released.

That kind of situation may happen only occasionally, or it may happen more than we realize. Whichever the case, it's important to know what is on your hands that could be transmitted to the fly. There are some commercial products that will disguise the alien smells that so abundantly surround our human life. Because the olfactory receptors are located on the front of the fish's head, you can bet that the trout will use this extraordinary power to its advantage when examining your fly, especially if it is out of the ordinary and doesn't conform to the criteria of the materials the fish is feeding on.

Sight

It's hard to say whether sound, smell, or sight is of greatest importance to fish. But it is sight that most fishermen concentrate on when they try to fool fish with a fly. We know that sight is important to the fish, for before it actually takes the food in its mouth it must see and accept it. Nevertheless, the water environment makes the fish's eyesight different from our own in important ways.

A trout's eyesight is quite acute, but its water environment limits the distances it can see clearly. It can distinguish movement from far away, but actual identification of that movement may be impossible. Where the trout excels is in its ability to focus at very close range—within an eighth of an inch. It is this ability that often explains a failed hookup when the fish has seemed to devour your fly. Slow-striking by the fisherman is not the cause; the fish has merely changed its mind and rejected the imitation at close range.

Fish can also make judgments based on color and profile. Behavioral research has shown that fish react to color, not merely primary colors, but subtle shades and hues. Coloration becomes insignificant only at the darkest part of the day, around midnight, when fish seem to see in shades of gray and black. Therefore, a fisherman who disregards color when selecting his fly is in for a big surprise.

THE TROUT'S "WINDOW"

All of a trout's food, on or in the water, is perceived through what is known as the trout's "window." Since the trout cannot see long distances, only food appearing within its viewing area gets its attention. The window is cone- or megaphone-shaped, extending from the eye upward at an ever-increasing diameter. The diameter of the circle at the surface will vary with the depth of the fish. The deeper the fish, the wider the cone; the shallower the fish, the narrower the visual cone.

Only when an item passes into that visual cone can a fish truly distinguish and inspect it. If the object is outside the cone, the fish may be alerted that something is floating toward it, but, again, only when the food actually floats downstream and enters the cone does the fish's sight take over. Thus, to

The Trout's "Window"

The deeper the fish is in the water, the larger its cone-shaped "window" of vision. Only when an object passes into this window can the fish inspect it.

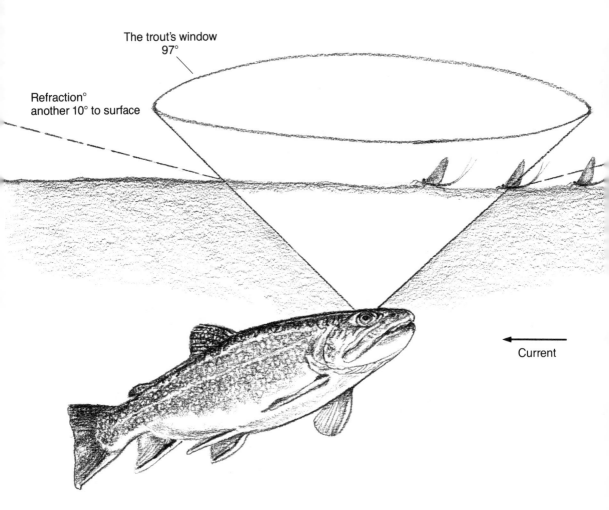

The trout's window
97°

Refraction°
another 10° to surface

Current

increase our chances of a strike, we must duplicate that natural sequence of activity in presenting our fly to the fish.

Once a fish, or a likely holding spot for fish, has been located, the inexperienced fisherman usually delivers his fly directly at that spot. Because the fly has not drifted naturally into the fish's field of vision, success is unlikely; the imitation has not arrived in the same manner as real food. The fisherman should therefore place his fly upstream of the fish's holding area and *allow the fly to float downstream into the visual cone, thus duplicating nature.*

The other senses, touch and taste, can be important to fish, but it is difficult to understand where one sense takes over from another. We do know that fish are extremely sensitive to the texture of a fly, natural or not. A hard-bodied artificial that looks technically correct often will be rejected, whereas a soft and fuzzy hoax will be more readily accepted. Here, touch has obviously influenced the fish.

Whatever you believe to be the most important of its senses, you must keep in mind that *all* the fish's senses are highly developed, subtle, instinctive, and adaptive, and that it constantly uses them to survive. Fishermen are just one, if perhaps the noisiest, smelliest, and most visible, of his enemies.

All right. We have examined the principal species of trout and how they use their senses for survival. Now we must look at where and why they locate themselves in a body of water. To overlook this aspect, despite everything else you know so far, will most certainly reduce your chances of success.

5

Reading and Approaching Fishable Water

To the inexperienced angler, reading or understanding fishable water can be both mysterious and confusing, but if you are to become successful with a fly, knowing the fish's environment is a must. Learning the unique characteristics of trout habitat means studying, observing, and actually fishing a stream. Eventually, you begin to "see" the water in terms of its potential for trout fishing.

In many ways, fly fishing is a sport learned through trial and error, especially with regard to reading water. Water is classified by fishermen into three basic categories: 1) flatwater or spring creeks, 2) lakes and ponds, and 3) freestone, or fast-moving, streams. In this chapter, we'll focus upon the most readable and most commonly fished water, that of freestone streams.

When one thinks of trout streams, it is the fast-moving, tumbling mountain versions that typically come to mind. Called "freestone" streams because their water moves freely and quickly over a stone or rock base, this fast-moving water yields areas of suitable shelter for fish to rest or remain stationary (hold). Before learning about these places, though, let's make sure we understand some things about the first ingredient to a stream's productivity: its water quality.

WATER QUALITY

The mere existence of water does not guarantee that it will be suitable for trout or for any other fish. Water may flow crystal-clear through a pristine setting, but if it lacks the necessary minerals and chemical and organic compounds, neither fish nor other aquatic life can flourish.

The ecology of a trout stream is a complex weave of interrelated elements.

Understanding where fish locate themselves within a stream is fundamental to fly-fishing success.

Spring creeks, such as this one in Pennsylvania, are normally rich in natural chemicals vital to fish and insect life.

Stream biologists consider a host of variables—dissolved oxygen, hydrogen sulfides, and nitrogen levels, for example—when determining the quality of water. All are important, but over the years I have found one factor to be of overriding importance to waterborn organisms, the *alkalinity level* of the water, or its measured *Ph factor.*

A stream's alkalinity is the measure of its concentration of calcium carbonate, a chemical usually formed from carbon dioxide and various limestone salts. The greater the concentration of calcium carbonate, the higher the alkalinity; the lower the concentration, the more "acid" the water. The more limestone found in the area where a stream drains, the stronger the likelihood that the stream can support aquatic life. Why?

Alkalinity is measured according to a Ph scale of 1 to 14, 7.0 being neutral, neither acid nor alkaline. Trout and other freshwater fish have an internal Ph slightly higher than 7.0. When water is highly acidic (the opposite of alkaline, which is called "soft water"), these fish use most of their bodies' energy trying to maintain a more neutral Ph balance. As a result, acid-type streams affect both fish growth and total population numbers, mostly for the worst. Aquatic insects follow the same course, which is one reason there is so much concern about acid rain and its effect on our waterways.

Streams with a Ph factor between 7.3 and 7.5, or hard water, are very precious. They are high-yield fish factories, producing dense populations of aquatic insects, which in turn are fed upon by thriving numbers of trout and other species. Classic examples of this type of water include the fabled chalk streams of England, the great Pennsylvania limestone waters, and the spring creeks of the northern Rockies.

As you can see, a stream's chemical content is vital to fish, but they have other, equally important, needs: namely, where they will live within the water system.

NEEDS OF FISH

Fish concern themselves with three fundamental needs: 1) security, 2) low current flow, and 3) food supply. These three elements will determine where they will locate themselves within a given waterway.

Security is of greatest importance to a fish. Over the course of the fish's life it is subjected to numerous dangers, mostly owing to its role as food for higher forms of life. It is only later in life, after it has grown large enough to be a victim in the old hook and line game, that fishermen join the fish's list of predators. During growth, fish do head-on battle with water scorpions, small mammals, snakes, and other fish. Winged danger from birds, such as blue herons, kingfishers, eagles, and osprey, is also omnipresent. Consequently, a trout's first concern is to locate a home that offers physical protection from all sides and from above.

Fish in a stream will also secure a place where the current is greatly reduced. Just like humans, a fish is naturally reluctant to fight the current, for, in its case, the energy needed to do so reduces its ability to perform other survival tasks.

Ideally, rather than moving for food, the fish locates itself where food continually goes to it. That means finding a spot where the *current* moves the food, though once again, the fish seeks a careful balance between the energy it must expend to hold in the current for its meal, and the meal itself. Security and current speed factors, always take precedence over food supply; though a fish can and will move to wherever a meal is being served, it will do so especially if the new spot is more advantageous.

A fish is territorial about its secure spots, or holding lies. It will protect its home, driving other fish away from the prime spot. Several fish can exist within a given hold, but the biggest fish will typically occupy the most advantageous locations.

All fish have a natural tendency to migrate, primarily for spawning and/or for a better food source. Most resist daily or weekly migration because, once again, the energy expended would be too great. Nevertheless, frequent migration does occur. On any day, fish may be driven out by other fish, or they may be caught and taken out by fishermen. Regardless of what causes a fish to abandon its hold, the space will quickly be taken over by another.

WATER DEPTH

Each stream, regardless of geographical location, has its own set of fingerprints, or characteristics, that make it unique. Actual on-stream experience is important for the newcomer, but there are some general stream characteristics that always indicate the possibility of good shelter for fish. Depth and reduced velocity, especially combined, are two of the most important.

Time and again I have found depth and depth changes to be significant indicators of holding water for fish. If we could view a stream in cross-section, we would see that water current works as logic would predict. Because air offers

Holding Locations of Fish
in Different Water Depths

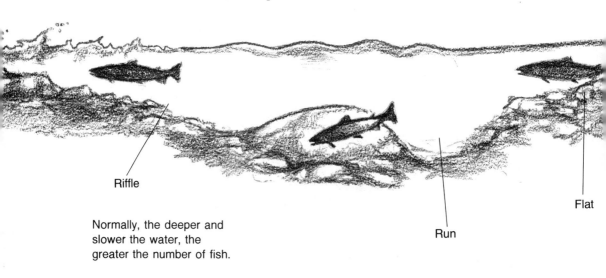

Riffle

Flat

Run

Normally, the deeper and
slower the water, the
greater the number of fish.

little resistance, the top layer of water has the fastest current. As we go deeper the current becomes slower. The very bottom is the slowest of all, owing to friction from the bottom itself. If there isn't sufficient depth (about two feet), fish will most likely not be found there.

However, depth alone does not always denote good holding water. Unless there is something to obstruct the swiftness of the river's flow, such as uneven rocks and boulders, depth can be useless. One season I fished a run of water that, to the eye, looked ideal for fish. It was a large run with a thigh-deep center. For the entire season, however, I was disappointed in both the number and the size of fish the pool produced. Finally, to relieve my curiosity and frustration, I donned a mask and snorkel to have a look at the pool from a fish's point of view. What I saw was an incredibly smooth streambed, with rocks of uniform size and type, providing absolutely no protection from the current. No wonder the pool was such a poor producer.

Now that you understand the importance of depth and water velocity to fish, let us define the four basic types of water that represent various degrees of depth: riffles, runs, pools, and flats.

Pool

RIFFLES, RUNS, POOLS, AND FLATS:
THE BIG FOUR

Fish hold in many places in a stream. Some are not easily detected by the inexperienced angler, but the big four—riffles, runs, pools, and flats—should be recognized and learned by every fisherman.

Riffles

A riffle is the fastest fishable water in a stream. It may be only knee-deep—perhaps two-and-a-half feet of water—but it is sufficient holding water for fish. What creates the riffle effect of the water is large rocks, either exposed or unexposed. The rocks obstruct the current and create the holding areas. Fishermen often refer to this type of water as "pocket water," and angling in it as "fishing the pockets." Depending upon the size of the stream, the pockets or "slicks" created by the obstructions can be small or quite large. But as great as this water is, it can create fishing problems for the angler.

Because the water is moving very quickly with erratic current changes, controlling the fly isn't easy. Short and/or direct upstream casts are often needed to control the speed of the fly as it passes through and over the holding water. Short casts allow you to lift the fly line over multiple crosscurrents, and upstream casts keep the fly in one continuous current. (More on these fishing techniques in Chapter Seven.)

Riffles.
This is generally the fastest fishable portion of a stream. With their small areas of smoother pocket water and slicks (both downstream of rocks), riffles are always worthwhile fishing spots.

Runs.
Runs are classic fly fishing locations. Coming off a riffle, or fast-water stretch, the stream both slows and deepens, making for an ideal trout habitat.

Runs

Because of the water speed created by a substantial gradient drop, a riffle often turns into a *run* of water, one of the most important water types in the river system. A run will be both deeper and slower moving than a riffle. First, the descending fast water erodes the bottom, adding depth to the area, and, second, because the bottom begins to flatten out, the current tends slow down.

A run is usually about waist-deep (three-and-a-half to four feet). Because the current has slowed measurably compared to the speed of a riffle, a run is a delight, not just for the fish, but also for the fishermen.

Another characteristic of a run is that one part, either the side or the middle, will be deeper and a bit faster than the rest. There will be a definite center current. Fish will hold both in the deepest part and in the shallower water next to this heavier center current.

Runs are the great classic water for all types of fishing. Because they are often numerous on a stream, good quantities of fish will hold throughout. Their current is less erratic than that of a riffle, so fly visibility and drift are not the problem that they are on faster water. Runs should be fished systematically, starting at the tail and moving upstream, fishing all parts.

As mentioned, runs of water are generally considered the premier fly water in a trout stream. With the possible exception of flats, a run is generally the maximum depth from which fish will feed to a surface imitation, regardless of a hatch. But there is deeper water still, and this we call a pool.

Pools

A pool is perhaps the most easily distinguished type of water, if for no other reason than that it offers a good swimming hole for non-anglers. It is created either by heavy plunging water, like a waterfall, or by a dramatic gradient drop that erodes the bottom to a depth of six feet or more. This depth eliminates many of the angling techniques employed on other types of water.

Fish are generally reluctant to move more than three-and-a-half to four feet upwards from the bottom to take aquatic surface insects. They will do so only when the hatch is significant enough—when there are insects of sufficient size or quantity—to warrant the energy expenditure necessary to intercept these tasty morsels. Therefore, more often than not, pools are best fished with weighted nymphs and possibly streamer imitations. A pool's depth may even require sinking-type fly lines—sink-tips or wetheads—for the angler to fully work the fish holding near the bottom.

In general, it is the slowed water and overall depth that make pools ideal holding water for trout. They should never be passed up.

Pools.
Deep pools are the most easily-distinguished holding waters. Because of their depth, they are often fished successfully with underwater fly patterns, such as nymphs and streamers (more later).

Flats.

Flats are characterized by shallow, slow-moving water, which must be approached cautiously lest you spook the fish. Lighter leaders, more precise imitations, and perhaps even a downstream presentation of the fly are often required (more on presentation later).

Flats

The last of the big four is the *flats*. As the name implies, these are large flat sections within an otherwise fast-moving stream. With little gradient drop in a flat, the water moves slowly, with minimal surface disturbance. Flats are generally even in depth from bank to bank, and relatively shallow throughout. A center current is not prominent as it is in a run of water.

Because the current is even and slowed, flats can become good stationing water for trout, especially while an insect hatch is in progress. Fish will move into these areas where they can easily locate and pick off the insects drifting about. But because of the shallower water and relatively undisturbed surface, the flats may not be the fish's primary shelter area. Caution should be the rule when approaching and fishing these areas.

Fishing flats requires care in casting and presenting the fly. The slower the water, the more easily trout can spot imperfections. Leader size can be significant and, because the surface is undisturbed, the fly itself must conform more closely to the natural.

You will quickly learn that runs, riffles, pools, and flats overlap each other, and it is sometimes difficult to distinguish where one begins and the other ends. Riffles can quite gently transform themselves into nice runs of water. And runs, especially in their tail sections, can develop into flats. But if you can learn to distinguish these four basic types of water you will be well on your way to adequately fishing most of the best areas in freestone streams.

In addition to the big four, there are other sections in a stream that hold fish and require specific techniques and considerations. River bends, undercut banks, fallen trees, islands, stream inlets, drop-offs, and back eddies are just a few.

OTHER FISHABLE STREAM SECTIONS

River Bends

Every river eventually makes turns, creating bends. These bends may be radical or gentle, but always they offer the strong likelihood of holding trout. Owing to water velocity, the deeper water will be to the outside of the bend, where the action of the current has eroded both bank and bottom. Larger fish gravitate to such spots. During a hatch, the fish may move into shallower water on the inside of a bend to feed, so care must be taken on approaching and fishing turns in the river.

To fish a bend, try taking up a position on the inside of the curve, fishing across to the deeper water. Standing on the outside bank puts the fish at your feet and a presented fly will tend to be swept toward you. It may not always be possible to reach the inside of the curve, especially in bigger rivers, but it should always be your goal.

Undercut Banks

Undercut banks are generally created by a radical bend in the river. They are excellent homes for fish. Not only is food being swept in to them, but security is assured by impenetrable overhead and side protection. Undercuts are typically found along oxbow-type streams that wind their way in serpentine fashion through meadows. Fish them from the inside portion, allowing the fly to be swept next to or into the undercut.

Banks don't have to be undercut to provide good trout habitat. Current is often slowed along any bank, and brush and trees afford the fish invaluable overhead protection. Food is also generated at streamside. For these reasons, you can bet that, if there is sufficient depth, the bank will be occupied by a fish. Note, however, that if the water is too shallow, all the other benefits of streamside living will not induce a fish to locate there.

Banks and overhanging trees.
Slow-moving water along a bank and overhead protection provided by trees and brush afford ideal holding water for trout.

Snags and Fallen Trees

Any place trees have fallen into a river system provides good fishing lies. The tree acts as an obstruction, very similar to a rock. The upstream portion of the tree, or snag, will slow the current, and if the tree is big enough it can create quite a substantial space. Below the snag, the water will slow dramatically, which all fish love. Unfortunately, when you hook a fish near a snag there is a good chance the fish will make macrame of your leader by weaving it around projecting branches. To avoid that, you must be craftier and more forceful than usual in working the fish out into open water. I have seen many a good fish escape in the tentacles of downed trees.

Rocks and boulders.
Fish hold not only near the downstream side of rocks and boulders, but often near the upstream side as well.

Islands

Islands are another fishable area in trout streams. Most are nothing more than very, very large rocks. The upstream portion of these obstructions creates an immense slackwater. Along the sides of the island the current will be slow, but is the most likely holding spot for trout is downstream of the island at the place where the two channels meet. Reasons: First, the two-current impact creates turbulence, which, in turn, erodes the bottom and adds depth; second, the opposing forces tend to neutralize one another, slowing the current. The downstream slackwater created by an island can in some cases extend a hundred yards downstream before the slowed water gathers steam once again. Never pass up islands, for they almost always hold fish.

Inlet or Side Streams

The place where smaller streams join larger ones is essential water for fish. An incoming stream can carry a higher water velocity, which will tend to dig out and erode the bottom, adding depths where fish may lie. And, as with islands, the joining currents will offset each other, slowing the water for some distance.

Inlets, or side streams.
Incoming streams usually deepen and neutralize the flow of the main stream at the point where the two intersect. Too, they offer an additional food source and, sometimes, cooler water, both desirable to trout.

There is also the matter of temperature. If the main stream tends to heat up in mid-summer, fish will congregate around inlets where the water is apt to be fresher and colder. The Firehole River in Yellowstone Park is a classic example. By August, the Firehole reaches temperatures that are uncomfortable for trout, and, as a result, the fish will move near inlets or even make their way up the sidestreams, seeking cooler water. Incoming streams can also bring in new types of food that fish may find succulent. Explore these waters thoroughly; they will hold trout.

Drop-offs

Fish love to congregate on, or just below, drop-offs. Either subtle or dramatic depth changes, drop-offs almost always are distinguishable by changes in the color of the water. In fishing them, I tell my customers to fish where the light water meets the dark. Drop-offs can be almost anywhere in a stream—along banks as well as at midstream. If the drop-off precedes a deep pool, most of the fish will be found on, or slightly upstream, of the drop-off itself. Present your fly above the drop-off and allow it to float into the pool. Generally, it is where the fly actually passes over the drop-off that the action will commence.

Back Eddies

Back eddies are generally situated along a bank and are caused by a heavy center current deflecting from an outcropping—a rock, a tree, or a point of land—and creating a circling effect behind the obstacle. Here the current will

Holding Locations
and Where to Fish Them

As this drawing shows, fish like to hold in many different locations along a stream or river. Here, the best locations for the angler to fish from are indicated by X's.

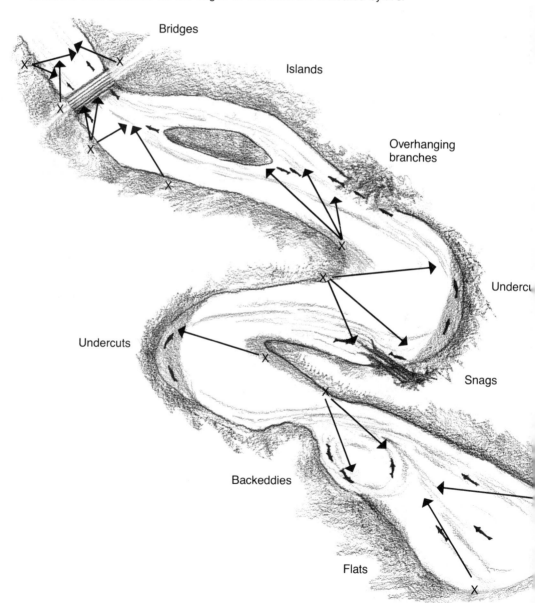

Bridges

Islands

Overhanging
branches

Undercu

Undercuts

Snags

Backeddies

Flats

actually flow upstream in a whirlpool. Back eddies almost always hold fish. It is important to realize that many of the fish in a back eddy will actually face downstream because the current will be flowing upstream. Present your fly below the fish and let the current carry it to him.

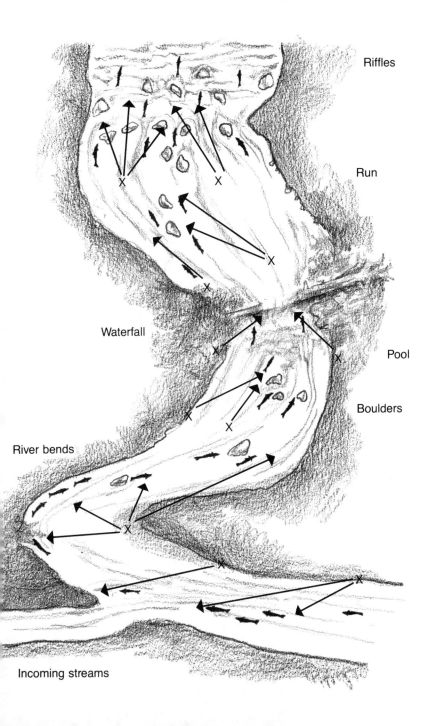

Riffles

Run

Waterfall

Pool

Boulders

River bends

Incoming streams

FISHING TECHNIQUE AND APPROACH

Whether or not you have located a prime piece of water or are an accomplished caster, all can be rendered useless if you do not fish your chosen water carefully and systematically. Regardless of the type of fly you use and the technique you employ, your fishing approach to the selected piece of water is critical.

In most cases, especially in fast water streams, you should approach the fish from *behind,* actually casting at various angles upstream. Fish face upstream to activate their gills more efficiently for oxygen, and to intercept food being carried toward them. Approaching from behind, you minimize the odds of being detected by the fish. Beyond this basic rule, you must now consider where to place your first, second, and third casts.

Anglers of all abilities tend to make a common but serious mistake. I call it the "grass is greener on the other side" syndrome. Walking into the stream, the angler will deliver his first cast, not in front of him, but completely across to the other bank. What this angler has just accomplished is to disturb every fish between himself and the opposite bank with his fly line. Don't do it!

To fish any location properly, approach from the tail or bottom portion and work toward the head. Before making a cast, analyze the holding water, pinpointing where you want to begin and where you will eventually finish up. You are identifying what I call the productive grid of water.

Visually divide your location into sections. If the pool is expansive, you can cut it into three, four, or five sections. Next, mentally impose a grid of two-foot squares onto each section. Your objective is to pass the fly over or through each and every square. Your first cast is short and directly in front of you. After thoroughly working those squares, extend the cast to the next group,

A

Fishing the Productive Grid

To improve your fishing success, mentally divide a stretch of productive water into a grid, and work it systematically, starting at the tail and the square of water nearest you (A). After working every square in that area, move upstream to the next section (B) and repeat the process, remembering to make your first cast to the nearest square and working outwards. In this sequence there are three sections. Depending on their size, water stretches can be divided into as many as ten sections, or as few as two.

and so on, until you have fished the entire section, before moving up to the next.

Another common mistake comes when a feeding fish is spotted in an upper section yet to be worked. Don't immediately begin casting to him, for again, you will spook all fish between you and the riser. *Stick to your game plan,* making a mental note of where the fish was feeding to be sure to cover that spot in your sequence. Obviously the fish likes the spot and will be there when you arrive.

After fishing the first section, move upstream (or in some cases downstream) to the next. The first cast is short, the next longer until you have completed all parts of that section.

As you can see, it is important to understand *where* fish are and how to approach those areas to maximize their potential. Novice anglers often waste time by devoting themselves to spots that will not be productive. Remember, *only a certain number of areas within a stream hold fish.* Also, you may have chosen one of the finest sections of the stream, but if you approach it haphazardly you will minimize your chances to succeed. From a section that could yield five, six, seven fish, the reckless fisherman is likely to take only one or two. Stop, observe, think, and *analyze* before entering the water. Your fishing will be much more satisfying if you do.

Now that you have some idea about where fish are and how to approach the water, it is time to learn what they feed on. Without this basic understanding, you will spend fruitless hours, regardless of how well you have mastered the cast or learned to read the water. To ignore what fish eat is perhaps the greatest mistake you can make, and, surprisingly, it's one even veteran anglers are often guilty of.

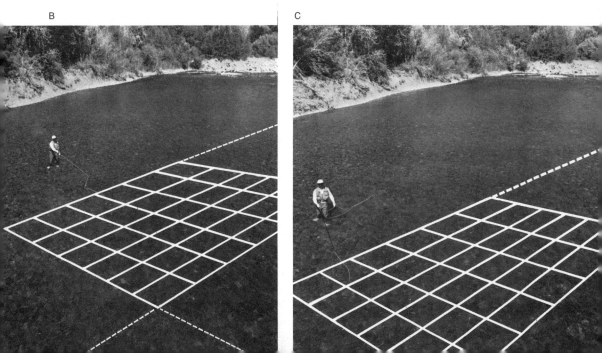

B   C

6

Food Sources

In my opinion, the real key to fly fishing success lies in understanding what fish feed on and what fly you can use to imitate those natural food species. Most aspects of fly fishing are fairly static. Equipment evolves slowly, and what was used 20 years ago may still be quite serviceable today. Fly casting is much like riding a bicycle: You might get a little rusty, but the technique never really leaves you. Streams may change because of flash floods or spring runoffs, creating new habitats while destroying others, but fish will still seek shelter in the same types of locations as they did before the stream change.

None of this can be said for the insect world. Although the habits and behavior of those insects that are the primary food sources of trout are some-what predictable, they are never static. The more one knows about insects and their world, the greater success one will have with fish. Sadly, I estimate that 70 percent of practitioners know little or nothing about this area, and, what is worse, couldn't care less.

For years, fly fishermen tended to resist the challenge presented by the profusion of insect life that surrounded their prey. Typically, the fisherman would select his fly based upon his own, or a friend's success, or even on a magazine article that recommended the latest imitations. Little attention was paid to what the fly actually imitated. If the fly worked, great; if it didn't, the fisherman would haphazardly try another of an estimated 30,000 fly patterns. The question of what was happening on, or in, the water was rarely asked. Today's angler should start by asking what and why; then, provided he or she has some knowledge of entomology, make a reasonable fly selection relating to the insect activity of the moment.

Many beginning fishermen mistakenly think that, for success, one needs to know all the scientific names and jargon associated with insects, not only

The adult mayfly is widely regarded as the Queen of the Trout Waters. Most conventional fly patterns are tied to imitate this insect. Note the upright wings, tapered body, and long, delicate tails: chief means of identifying the mayfly.

locally but throughout the entire fly fishing world. That is nonsense. Knowing what the prevailing insects in their various stages look like is far more important. Eventually, the Latin names of species can be helpful, for they provide a common language with which fishermen can exchange information, but as a beginner or intermediate fly fisherman, you needn't worry about the scientific names yet. Instead, your main concern should be in identifying insects, and understanding their life cycles and the various stages within those cycles. Nothing more.

In studying trout foods (insects, primarily) anglers concern themselves with those that are aquatic (spend their life in a water environment) and those that are terrestrial (land-based). Each is important.

AQUATIC INSECTS

Aquatic insects represent the largest food group in the diet of freshwater fish. They exist in great numbers, and their abundance ensures their availability to the fish in one stage or another. In its own way, the fish both knows and understands each type and stage of an insect's life. Therefore it makes good sense for you to know these stages, too.

Generally speaking, all aquatic insects have an underwater stage, referred to as the *nymphal* or *larval stage,* and an adult, or actual flying, stage. There are many orders of aquatic insects, each with its own peculiarities. To examine all would be unnecessary and confusing. Instead, let's look at the main types that make up some 75 percent of the fish's diet.

The Mayfly

The mayfly is perhaps the most important—certainly the most written about—of all aquatic insect orders. Many fishing entomology books have devoted the greater part of their pages to this majestic and beautiful insect. More than any other type, the mayfly is entitled to be called "Queen of the Waters".

Mayflies are relatively small insects, ranging from three millimeters to about 25 mm, or about one inch, in length. There are literally hundreds of different species throughout the world, but what prevails in one country may not be found in another, and what exists in one region of a country may be absent in another. Since many of the flies are similar in coloration and of course

A typical mayfly nymph.
Mayfly nymphs are best identified by their six legs, two or three tails, abdominal gills on the sides and tops of their bodies, and single wing pads.

profile, an artificial pattern used in one area could very well work in another, requiring only a change in size for success.

The mayfly's lifespan generally covers about one year, and 99 per cent of the time is spent in the water. From an egg, it quickly develops into a nymph stage, consuming smaller life forms and growing slowly until it reaches maturity—roughly a year from the time the eggs were deposited. Because there are millions upon millions of mayfly nymphs, and because of a phenomenon called "continual drift," or daily downstream movement, these creatures are constantly being presented to hungry fish over the course of a year. Nymphs therefore constitute the greatest single food source of the trout, and thus are important as an imitative stage for the fly fisherman.

Upon reaching maturity, at a particular hour within a day, some of the surviving nymphs of a given species will lift off the bottom and struggle to the surface to hatch. Splitting out of their nymph cases, they emerge as fully formed, winged adult mayflies. This first adult stage is referred to as the *dun stage* because the upright wings themselves are dun or gray in color.

The dun is important to fly fishermen because it quickly invites surface feeding by the fish. The fragile mayfly remains on the water's surface until its wings become aerodynamic enough for flight. To the trout waiting below, these vulnerable creatures represent an easy meal. To the angler waiting above, this stage represents perhaps the greatest delight of the sport—dry fly fishing (more later).

The duns not ending up in the stomach of fish will lift gracefully from the water and proceed immediately to the bank, where they undergo a second metamorphosis, unique to the mayfly, during which they shed their minutes- or hours-old identity and pass on to the final mating, or *spinner stage*.

Anywhere from 30 minutes to 24 hours after reaching this second adult stage, the mayflies gather over the stream or lake in clouds for mating. Each female will descend grasping a male from above, with actual mating taking place in mid-air. After conception, both insects fall to the water, where the female deposits her newly fertilized egg mass. Spinner activity is noticeable when clouds of mayflies form over the water, and a vivid up-and-down flight movement is performed by both insects. After death, which happens very soon after the fly hits the water, the on-the-water profile of the mayfly spinner changes from the upright wing of the dun to a flat, laid out or "spent" winged outline. This *spent-spinner stage* is, of course, important, from both a fishing and a fly imitation standpoint.

The adult life of these insects is extremely short. The order of mayflies *Ephemeroptera* derives its name from the insects' "ephemeral" or "short lived" existence. Propagation is the only purpose of the adult stage, for the adult does not have mouth parts for eating. Fortunately for trout fishermen, these stages last just long enough for us to enjoy some of our grandest moments.

The Caddisfly

The caddisfly comes from the order *Trichoptera*. Even though these insects are the subject of few published texts and have never been as popular an imitation as the mayfly, the caddis is extremely important to our sport. Like the mayfly, the caddis has hundreds of different species, and because the eggs are deposited in such great numbers, it represents a primary food source for fish.

The caddis differs from the mayfly in that its entire metamorphosis takes place under the water. From an egg, it transforms into a larva, or wormlike stage, which takes one of three forms: It builds what is known as a caddis-case

The Caddis

The next most important food for trout is the caddis, often called a grandom or a sedge. Characterized by its tent-like wings, the caddis is the primary trout food in many streams.

 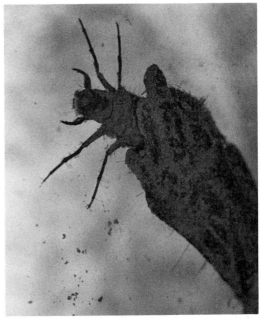

Caddis larva.
Two different typical caddis larvae: freeswimming (left) and case (right). Caddis larvae are chiefly identified by their wormlike appearance, the presence of their six legs behind the head, and their lack of visible wing pads, antennae, and tails.

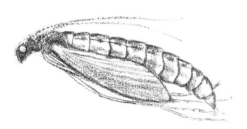 

Caddis pupa.
This is the form the caddis assumes as it begins its rise to the water's surface. Its chief identifying points are its six long legs, two long antennae, and two wing pads on the sides of the main body.

Caddis adult.
The best way to identify a caddis adult is by the tentlike profile of its wings. An adult caddis's flight somewhat resembles a moth's.

around its body, it swims freeform, attaching itself to weeds by a fine silk strand, or it constructs a tiny net structure between rocks to catch its food.

Case-makers construct their houses out of microscopic debris, particles of sand or organic material available in the waterways they inhabit. The larva stays within this case throughout its larval stage, the case expanding as larval growth occurs. Because these cased caddis—often called periwinkles or rock rollers—do not particularly lend themselves to movement within the stream (they often attach to rocks or other debris), they have not proved to be a very successful model for fishermen to imitate. Duplicating them visually presents no problem, but mimicking their movement (or non-movement) in the water is difficult. The free-swimming caddis-larva is a better bet for fishermen. This unattached, worm-like larva drifts slowly near the bottom of the stream. A good imitation successfully mimics this delectable morsel.

As a caddis larva begins to mature, it either closes off its little case, or, if a free swimmer, makes a small cocoon around itself, to complete its metamorphosis to the adult stage. At full maturity—called the *pupa stage*—the caddis traps air bubbles in its case and rapidly makes its way to the surface. This rapid upward movement induces slashing and charging rises from the trout that sometimes signal the angler that caddis pupa are on the move. From a back eddy, I once observed caddis pupa hatching and noted that the speed of the rise from bottom to top was comparable to the speed of a released cork rising from the bottom of a bathtub. This rising stage is *the* most important of the underwater stages of caddis for the fly fisherman.

Upon reaching the surface, the pupa sheath splits open and the *adult stage* immediately lifts off the water. In profile, the adult's wings lie tentlike over its body—a much different profile than that of a mayfly. In flight, the caddis somewhat resembles a moth. Flying to the bank, it remains there perhaps two or three days before mating in the vegetation. After mating, it returns to the water to deposit the eggs, again becoming a likely meal for fish.

In general, I have always found the greatest activity in the caddis in late afternoon or early evening. I have seen them by the millions doing their life-and-death dances over streams teeming with hungry trout. Because caddis are very prevalent and important insects, fishermen should carry at least a few of the imitative patterns that suggest the natural. To forget the caddis is to leave a large gap in a well-rounded fly box.

The Stonefly

The stonefly is the third most important of the aquatic insects. *It's important to remember, however, that there is no real hierarchy among insects. Each type—mayfly, caddis, stonefly, or others—has its moment when the trout concentrate on it as a food source. It's just that, because of their numbers, some insects have more moments than others.*

Stoneflies are unique in that they must locate themselves in fast-water streams. Although a relatively small order of insects, the stonefly becomes extremely important to the angler at certain times of the year, and its overall size range—seven mm to over 50 mm in length—ensures the attention of even the largest fish in the streams.

The stonefly has two stages, nymph and adult. As a nymph, it may remain underwater from one to three years, depending on the species. The larger species generally have longer lifespans. At various times of the year the nymphs are very abundant, and, because they crawl and cling rather than swim about,

Typical stonefly nymph.
Nymphs are easily identified by their two wing pads, or cases, two antennae and tails, and fuzzy gill hairs, or filaments, surrounding their six legs.

Typical stonefly adult.
Adults can be identified by their double wings folded over the top of the body, their large antennae, and twin, widely separated tails.

they become fairly helpless if detached from the streambed. Thus, fish will readily grab a good fly imitation that is allowed to dead-drift (more on this technique later) through good holding water.

On its day of maturity, instead of floating to the surface like the mayfly and caddis, the stone fly crawls out of the water onto rocks, trees, or the bank and splits out of its case, leaving behind an exterior skeleton often observed by fishermen. The adult may live on the bank for three to five days before mating farther up on the land, after which it flies back to the water, where it deposits some 10,000 eggs, and thus, again, becomes important to both fish and fisherman.

Its importance increases with its size. The East has its giant Perla stones, while the West boasts hatches of both the Golden and the famous Salmon flies. What makes these unique among all aquatic hatches is that the flies reach 50 mm in length—about the length of an adult man's little finger. Insects so large often attract eight-to-ten pound trout that otherwise remain on the bottom, feeding on either nymph or fish forms.

The stonefly also comes in smaller sizes, in both the East and the West. Early brown and black stoneflies occur throughout the country. In the West the brightly colored yellow stones, often referred to as "yellow Sallys" or "Mormon girls," are abundant enough to provide good fishing activity for all fishermen.

Wherever stoneflies exist they should be fished diligently. Their overall size, both in adult and nymph stages, makes them ideal food for fish. You should be armed with some stonefly patterns, especially if freestone water is your fare.

Midges

Depending upon location, midges can be a major food source for fish. They can exist by the billions and can take precedence over all other aquatic insects. The midge falls into the immense order of *Diptera,* or True Flies, an order containing gnats, mosquitoes, craneflies, and many others.

Midges are found primarily in the slow-moving waters of lakes, ponds, or spring creeks, but can also be found within the slower sections of freestone water. In general, midges are very small in size and for that reason are often overlooked by the unobservant angler. Like the caddisfly, the midge has a larva stage which looks like a thread-shaped worm on the bottom of a stream. At maturity the larva pupates, drifts, and hangs just below the surface of the water before emerging as an adult.

Midges

Midge larva.
These simple creatures are best identified by their wormlike bodies and lack of a visible head, body, or tail.

Midge adults.
The adult midge is best identified by its mosquito-like profile and single pair of rounded wings, which are shorter than the body.

All midge stages can be important to the angler, but most fishermen concentrate on the pupa and adult stages. Pupa imitations are tied with very thin bodies and a bulbed head and are fished on long leaders just underneath the surface. The adult will also remain on the surface for some length of time, making it an important dry fly model. Because of their quantity, adult midges often congregate tightly together, creating small balls on the surface. Trout will often choose to concentrate their feeding on these masses, rather than taking one fly at a time.

Anglers are often surprised and fooled to see fish actively pursuing such small insects, passing up larger and more delectable aquatics, such as mayflies and caddis. Recognizing midge activity is important, therefore, especially in slow-water situations when either nothing of consequence appears on the water or, again, very visible aquatic insects are not being fed upon while fish are continually rising. If you look carefully at water surface, you will probably find midges. Your imitation should be fished precisely in terms of size and profile.

There are many, many other aquatic insects of importance, the most significant of which are found in lakes and ponds. These will include damselflies, dragonflies, alder flies, and the non-insect form of leeches and freshwater shrimp. Because they mainly inhabit still water we will discuss them in more detail in the chapter on lakes and ponds.

TERRESTRIAL INSECTS

Aquatic insects are the trout's primary food, but there are times during the latter summer months when terrestrial insects become important, too. Terrestrials don't live or breed in water, but are land-based and become available to fish when they fall or are blown into the water. In the eastern United States, where most aquatic hatches end by midsummer, terrestrials may become the main food source for fish. In the West, hatches last throughout the summer, but, because terrestrials are in great abundance, they are expected and sought out by fish.

Included in the category of terrestrials are a variety of ants and beetles, the green oakworm of the East, and—the most universal of all terrestrials— grasshoppers and leafhoppers. After landing on a water surface, terrestrial insects are unable either to fly or to lift themselves away, and thus become vulnerable prey for trout.

Fishing grasshoppers can be an exciting and rewarding experience. The fly is large enough to attract big fish, and because the imitation is easily seen on the water and can be crudely presented, it is easily fished by anglers of all abilities. In fact, many times a sloppily presented fly will get the best results.

The knowledgeable angler should carry a full array of terrestrial imitations in various sizes. A fly box should contain both black and cinnamon ants, in flying and non-flying stages, leafhoppers and grasshoppers, black beetles and, if you fish in the northeastern United States, green oakworms. I always carry a few terrestrials with me and have found they can make the difference between success and failure in some highly selective trout waters.

BAITFISH

Once a fish reaches a length of perhaps 15 inches, it begins to supplement its diet with other fish. When a fish reaches a very large size, its cuisine may consist solely of other fish. Referred to as forage or bait fish, the edible types are endless: dace, shiners, the alevian of the Great Lakes, chubs, small perch, the very important bullheads, or sculpins, and, of course, other trout. Flies used to imitate fish are referred to as streamers, for they are tied in such a manner that when wet they flow backward, forming the outline of a baitfish.

To give you an idea of the gluttonous attitude of some fish toward baitfish: I once had a customer catch an 18-inch trout and elect to kill it for breakfast. Upon netting the fish, we found the tail of a five-inch-long sculpin protruding

Terrestrials

Ants.

Ants are an important food source, sometimes preferred by trout over all others. Many times, an ant imitation will catch fish when all other fly patterns have failed.

Beetles.

Various species of beetles, when found in abundance, are another important trout food. Always carry a few imitations in different sizes when you go on stream.

Grasshoppers.

The grasshopper is the king of the terrestrials. Grasshopper imitations in various sizes often take large fish.

Baitfish.
Larger trout supplement their diet with baitfish, such as the sculpin, shown here.

from its mouth—a robust meal in itself for a fish that size. Upon cleaning the fish, we found 18 undigested large stoneflies. And yet, with all this food, some still not even swallowed, it had taken a large stonefly imitation! Where the fish planned to put this latest morsel I haven't the foggiest idea.

If you are looking strictly for larger fish, fishing a bait imitation, or streamer, should definitely be considered. Large fish spend their time concentrating on other fish as food, and you should give them what they want.

HATCH CHARACTERISTICS

Throughout this book, I have continually referred to "the hatch," but, to many beginning fly fishermen, the term can be somewhat confusing and ambiguous. In specific terms, a hatch is the actual hatching of an adult insect. But, generally speaking, the term refers to any activity or movement of insect stages above or below the surface of the water. Hatching activities are as inevitable as the seasons and therefore somewhat predictable; we use this predictability as a means of deciding when and where we want to fish.

All aquatic insect species have their ecological niche. As part of the orderliness of nature, each species appears not only during a certain part of the year but at certain times of the day. A "hatch" may last for two or three hours or, if the weather is inclement, for an entire day. Also, hatches of one particular species may appear every day for two to six weeks before completing their yearly cycle. In addition, different hatches of different species can be sequential, overlapping, or simultaneous with others.

A fishable hatch requires insect *quantity*. Although there is no absolute minimum, generally hundreds of insects must appear on the water before fish will feed. While entomologists may get excited about one insect of a rare species, fish are only interested in those that appear in plenty. *A curiosity, therefore, is not a fishable fly.*

The mechanism that triggers an insect hatch is somewhat mysterious and not fully understood. Obviously, insect maturation is involved, but water temperature and air humidity can also be factors. An insect has a refined apparatus for detecting the slightest change in air or water temperature and barometric pressure. This unique registering system can either cause a hatch to stall until more favorable conditions develop, or speed its timetable.

During early spring and summer when air and water are often cool, most hatches will commence in early afternoon or at the warmest part of the day. As summer progresses toward its highest temperatures, midday air temperatures can be too hot, with hatches shifting to morning or early evening. Surprisingly, though, it appears to be the *humidity* of these periods rather than the water temperature that stimulates these shifts. Many entomologists now theorize that nymphs as well as adults have trouble emerging from their cases or their exoskeletal skins without a certain moisture content in the air. Therefore, during the heat of late summer little hatch activity will be found between noon and, say, five o'clock when the air is insufficiently humid.

Weather can also trick insects into hatching. If a heavy afternoon thunderstorm appears, severely darkening the sky, the insects may register that evening has arrived and begin their emergence. While there is heavy overcast or drizzling rain, hatching can occur throughout the day, especially if the hatching species is known to emerge in late afternoon.

We are fortunate to know something about what causes insect activity. Our guidelines are at best general rules, but they do allow us to chart the fishing season with reasonable assurance that a particular hatch or hatches will occur within a general period of time. Without this predictability, fishing a hatch would be a crap shoot at best.

Multiple and Complexed Hatches

Multiple and complexed hatches present the greatest problems to fishermen. The task is always easiest if just one natural species is on the water and the choice of imitation is obvious. But when several species of one particular type of fly (multiple), or two or more different orders (complexed), are hatching at once, determining the fish's choice can be difficult.

When two different mayflies of distinctly different sizes appear on the water, the inexperienced angler naturally chooses the larger fly, figuring it is easier to see and fish obviously prefer the greater food content. I have fished hatches where the very large mayflies, the western Green Drakes, were present, but the much smaller Pale Morning Dun *(Ephemerella)* was there in greater profusion and the larger specimen was completely ignored. As a rule, *select the fly that is present in the greatest quantity; quantity takes precedence over size.*

In a complexed hatch you may have a mayfly species emerging, a mayfly spinnerfall dropping to the water, caddis depositing their eggs, and a host of midges delicately riding the current. Many times, trial and error must be the rule, but if you can detect the quantity factor, or visually observe what the fish are taking, you can eliminate some of the possibilities.

Stillborn activity has recently been recognized as an important factor in aquatic hatching activity overall. The term applies to a hatching insect that, in trying to free itself of its nymphal shuck, or case, gets trapped. Fish quickly realize that these forms will not fly away and they key on these cripples rather than on the fully developed adult flies. All aquatic orders have stillborn activity, and various flies are tied to imitate this condition. Therefore, especially on selective waters, stillborn is not a category to be ignored by the serious angler.

FINDING WHAT FISH ARE FEEDING UPON

Now that you have learned at least the basic foods of fish, the obvious question arises as to how one finds out what fish are in fact feeding upon. The first and certainly most obvious and simplest method, is observing what insect is on or flying about the water itself. If an unknown or an undistinguishable insect has flown to the bank, it is often wise to walk over and examine the adult for size, coloration, and type. When insects are found or seen on the water, you can easily collect samples by using a small aquarium net carried in the vest. For both immediate and long-term research, actual seining of the river system helps to identify not only insects that are presently hatching but also those species of insects that live within the river system in quantity and are very close to maturity and thus hatching. Seining the river is somewhat laborious but can be accomplished by attaching fine mesh, such as window screening, to two poles or stakes, pushing the stakes into the streambed, and then kicking up the bottom just upstream of the net itself.

One of the most frustrating situations in the world of fly fishing is when you have feeding fish in front of you and can't identify or see what the fish are eating, especially in freestone water. One very quick and easy method of solving the mystery is to check small backwaters, eddys, and small side pools of water where insects tend to collect. Many times these areas identify not only what is presently taking place but also what might have taken place earlier in the day or on previous days. And, finally, perhaps the most effective method in identifying insects, or more precisely what the fish has been feeding upon, is to check the actual content of the fish's stomach and esophagus. This is done *not by killing the fish,* but rather by pumping its stomach, using a simple, syringe-type stomach pump. This delightful gadget is easy to operate and does not harm the fish. Rather, it efficiently relieves the fish of its morning or afternoon meal. Many times you will be surprised and enlightened at what you find using this device.

How to Determine What Fish Are Feeding Upon

Look in the air.
Being able to recognize various insects in flight is a crucial skill for the serious fly fisherman. Often, the answer to what the fish are feeding upon is in the air around you.

Look in trees and bushes.
Examples of both aquatic and terrestrial insects that fish might be feeding upon can often be found in the streamside greenery.

How to Determine What Fish are Feeding On (Cont.)

Look in shallows.
Both during and after a hatch, small side pools and back eddies are a good source of information about insect activity.

Use a seine.
A simple seine, made with short poles and fine netting, is an excellent tool for helping to determine which nymphs and hatching insects are present underwater.

Look under rocks.
Even without a seine, you can discover the nymph species present in a stream by examining a few rocks from the stream bed.

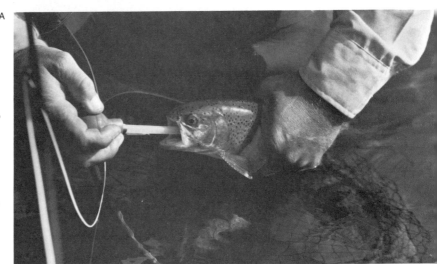

A

Use a stomach pump.
A stomach pump allows you to examine a fish's diet without killing the fish. When using one, first squirt a tiny amount of water into the fish's stomach, then suck out the stomach's contents (A). Reload the pump with water, squirt the contents into your hand and observe (B). Always clean the pump afterwards.

B

FLY IMITATION RATIONALE

All else being equal, having made an adequate cast and presented the fly properly, you want a consistent fly pattern, that is, one that works 90 per cent of the time. Unfortunately, many anglers are ignorant of entomology and have not observed what fish are feeding on, and thus concentrate on a fly that, all too often, hasn't been especially successful.

Most fly fishermen fall into two categories: those who are solely *pattern-conscious* and those who *first analyze what is on the water before going to their fly boxes.* The pattern-conscious fishermen concentrate their selections on a small group of flies they have carried over the years, regardless of what these old standbys imitate. As mentioned earlier, their information is obtained from past successes, friends, or magazine articles claiming that the fly will work under any conditions. Alas, life is never so easy. I once went fishing with a gentleman on his home waters, and when I politely asked him what pattern he was going to use he told me, "Mr. Mason, I put an Adams on 30 years ago and I haven't taken it off since." Now, the Adams happens to be a very good general-use fly, but with that attitude the angler limits himself to just one of the countless species that do exist and are fed on by fish. I remember another elderly gentleman who told me, "If they don't want a Royal Wulff, they can damn well go hungry." Again, in both cases, such an attitude dramatically limits the opportunities to take fish, especially in a selective hatch situation.

In matching a hatch, there are criteria we should follow, especially if we are fishing a dry fly. They include *size, profile,* and *color.*

MATCHING THE HATCH

Size

Size is the most important fly characteristic that anglers can duplicate. Forced to choose, I would rather have the appropriate size of fly than its exact profile or matching color. Fish understand size, and the smaller the natural fly, the more exacting the fish's judgment. Granted, small flies can be troublesome to see, and we tend to cheat a bit with larger imitations than the natural. But, for the most part, we end up cheating ourselves, because the trout know the difference. What often appears extremely small, and therefore close enough, to us will be passed up by fish who are looking for a more specific size.

Very large flies can also be a problem. What logically appears irresistible to us may be just plain suspicious to fish. A hatch of very large mayflies, caddis, or stoneflies does not necessarily mean that the fish will automatically begin to feed on it. These flies represent something so uniquely big that apprehension

Matching the hatch: size, profile, and color.
Once you've determined what's hatching, find an imitation whose size, profile, and color match it.

is the trout's first reaction. It is only after a few days of random feeding that the fish, having sampled the hatch thoroughly, will become reckless in their approach to an imitation.

Fish also have short memories. If an insect is not seen or has disappeared from the area, fish will soon forget it. Fish need constant reinforcement. I once guided a gentleman who had had great success with grasshoppers in August. He returned the following June for more of the same, but, because hoppers were not out, he caught nothing. He quickly changed his thinking about his choice of fly. Size is important; your fly must conform as closely as possible to the size of whatever is being eaten that day, or that moment, or you, too, will catch very little.

Profile

Different insects have their own distinct profiles as they appear on or in the water, and these silhouettes are of great significance to fish. Mayfly duns appear with an upright wing, but the spinners of the mayfly are often laid out flat, in what is known as a *spent position*. The caddis folds its wings into a tent over its body, and the stonefly has its own way of flattening its wings when not yet spent. Trout understand these profile changes, so naturally we tie flies in shapes that match them. To ignore profile is to ignore an element fundamental to fly imitation.

Color

Years ago, color was given more credence than it presently is. A close color match is usually good enough, so long as size and profile are met. Coloration is pretty much in the eye of the beholder, or flytier. Ten people might sit down to a flytying vise to produce a replica of a natural specimen found on the water, and six different color combinations probably would result. One person might see more yellow where another sees a bit more olive; a touch of gray might be the predominant hue seen by a third person. In all likelihood, all three will work if size and profile are correct. The key here is to *select a fly color that is as close to the natural as possible.*

There is a staggering number of fly patterns available today, many of which are very close in coloration. Therefore, the beginning angler should choose a simple selection that first meets the basic color of most insects—gray, cream, olive, brown. After selecting a fly pattern, he should then purchase them in a variety of sizes that can meet onstream requirements. Although I dislike the pattern-conscious approach, the following is a basic selection of flies that an angler will need for success.

BASIC FLY ASSORTMENT

Standard Dry Flies

Adams #12, #14, #16, #18, #20
Light Cahill #14, #16, #18, #20
Light Hendrickson #14, #16, #18, #20
Gordon Quill #12, #14, #16, #18, #20
Red Quill #14, #16, #18, #20

Tan Elkhair Caddis #12, #14, #16
Olive Elkhair Caddis #12, #14, #16
Little Yellow Stone #12, #14
Little Black Stone #12, #14
Hemingway Caddis #14, #16, #18

Hairwing Flies (for very fast water)
Royal Wulff #12, #14, #16, #18
Gray Wulff #12, #14, #16
Grizzly Wulff #12, #14, #16
Yellow Humpy #12, #14, #16, #18

Nymphs

Gold-Ribbed Hare Ear #10, #12, #14, #16
Prince Nymph #10, #12, #14
Otter Shrimp #10, #12, #14, #16
Tan Caddis Pupa #12, #14, #16
Olive Caddis Pupa #12, #14, #16

Green Caddis Larva #12, #14, #16
Zug Bug #12, #14, #16
Olive Woolly #8, #10, #12, #14
Brown Woolly #8, #10, #12, #14
Black Woolly #8, #10, #12, #14

Terrestrials

Black Ant #14, #16, #18
Black Flying Ant #14, #16, #18
Cinnamon Ant #14, #16, #18

Crowe Beatle #14, #16, #18
Dave's Hopper #8, #10, #12, #14
Green Oakworm #14, #16 (Eastern U.S.)

Streamers

Muddler Minnow #4, #6, #8, #10, #12
Light Spruce #4, #6, #8
Dark Spruce #4, #6, #8

Black Marabou #4, #6, #8
Black Woolly Bugger #2, #4, #6, #8
Olive Woolly Bugger #2, #4, #6, #8

Note that the above list is only a general guide. When in an unfamiliar area, you should always check with the local fly shops for advice. The people there know what is hatching and effective, as well as where and when. Local consultation can be your greatest ally.

7

Fishing Technique

If the fly is not presented properly to the fish, all the money in the world invested in costly equipment and flies, and all the hours spent perfecting your casting technique, will not improve your chances of catching fish. Time and time again, fishermen with the correct pattern for a given situation have little success, most often because their technique did not meet the standards that the fly called for. The fish, you must understand, is unimpressed as to whether the fly is gold-plated or tied by the most skilled craftsman in the world. If the fly does not act as its natural counterpart does while on or in the water, it will be rejected. In this chapter, our aim is learning correct presentation of a fly.

Remember how a trout views its food in its water environment, through its "window" or field of vision? As you will recall, trout do not see great distances. They only visualize and focus on food when it enters or drifts into their cone-shaped window, extending from the eye to the surface. Therefore, regardless of whether you fish a surface or subsurface fly, you must duplicate the situation by presenting your morsel upstream of the fish or its lie, allowing it to float down into view. That is the natural sequence of events to the fish. Presenting the fly directly at a rising trout, or to his holding spot, will all too often produce no results because, once again, the fly did not arrive as a natural insect would. Proper line drift is important, but so is how the fly appears to the fish when entering its field of vision.

DRAG AND CORRECTIVE MENDING

All streams have multiple currents. Between yourself and the target area, faster or slower water current will be found; seldom will you find a stream with current equal from bank to bank. These multiple currents play havoc with the

Selecting the right fly is important, but even the best fly, if not fished properly, will fail to bring success.

fly. The uneven water speeds either push or pull on your fly line, creating a "belly" in it, which, if allowed to remain on or in the water, will ultimately drag or skate the fly across or through the water. Since such movement, for the most part does not conform to natural insect behavior, you must manipulate the line to prevent or eliminate this belly and drag. In other words, you must learn to "mend" your line so that the fly travels at exactly the same speed as the current into which it has been cast—no faster, no slower.

The Upstream Mend

If, as is most often the case, fast water lies between you and your target area after you've made your cast, the line belly will quickly form downstream of where the fly lands. With your rod in hand, flip and roll the rod and line back upstream, to eliminate the belly.

The Downstream Mend

Many times your target is in fast water, while the water between you and it is slow. The fly lands and quickly begins to float downstream. However, the

The Upstream Mend

Use the upstream mend when fast water lies between you and your target area. As soon as the line starts to belly downstream of the fly (A), roll the rod upstream (B). This, in turn,

A

B

Current

slower current soon slows the line, which forms a belly and restrains the fly's movement downstream. To counter this form of drag, you must now roll and flip the rod in a downstream direction so that the fly is free to travel at the quicker current's speed. In general, mending is a matter of watching the belly of the line. *Roll the line in the direction opposite to the way the belly is forming.*

A final note on fly line drag problems: As you progress with your fishing, you will learn to anticipate drag problems before they happen. Upon entering a good run of water, first look at the current and decide what drag problem you are likely to encounter. With practice you will find yourself mending your line before bellies and drag become a problem, which, in turn, will mean catching more fish. Such advance planning will give you a better chance to fool the fish the first time, when he is most vulnerable, rather than the third time, when he may be slightly suspicious.

There are four types of flies we can use to take fish in a stream: 1) the dry fly, or surface type fly; 2) the wet fly, which is fished subsurface; 3) a nymphal imitation, (also fished subsurface); and 4) the streamer, (subsurface, too). Each has its place and requires a different fishing technique that should be part of a successful angler's repertoire.

will roll the line upstream (C), eliminating the belly (D). Note: You may have to mend more than once to maintain a drag-free float.

C

D

A   B

The Downstream Mend

A fly line that lands in water moving slower than where the fly lands can cause the fly to stall in the current rather than drift naturally with it (A). To eliminate the upstream line belly

THE DRY FLY

To many non-anglers, fishing the dry fly is what the sport of fly fishing is all about. Unfortunately, some fly fishermen regard dry fly fishing as the *only* way to fish, and approach it as a near-religious experience. I happen to think they're wrong—fishing other fly types can be just as satisfying, and in the case of nymph fishing, as we'll see, even more delicate an art than dry fly fishing. But I understand these purists' enthusiasm: The ability of the fisherman to *see* the action take place—to actually see the trout take the fly right before the fisherman's eyes—does make the dry fly an addictive technique.

The dry fly is an imitation of either an aquatic or a terrestrial insect in the adult stage that rides the surface of the water, making itself accessible to the trout. The fly is tied in a manner to mimic its counterpart in size, profile, and color. Since the way the fly rides the currents must duplicate a real insect's movements, a few techniques must be learned to mirror nature. They are all needed for successful dry fly fishing.

Fishing a dry fly requires no special equipment. The same rod and reel you use for your other techniques will work fine. Rods were once classified as either stiff, (dry fly action), or soft, (wet fly action). The stiff, dry fly rods provided

C   D

caused by the slower current, roll your arm and wrist downstream (B). This, in turn, will roll the line upstream (C), eliminating the belly (D). Be prepared to mend again for longer drag-free drift.

a quick action for striking a rising fish and a better responsiveness during the numerous false casts often required to dry the fly. Today, a medium-action rod will suffice for both surface *and* subsurface fishing.

Dry flies are generally tied from naturally buoyant materials. In addition, to facilitate floatation, they are constructed on very light wire hooks treated with a silicon ointment. Of course, to maintain buoyancy, they must be fished with a floating, rather than a sinking, fly line.

There are various methods used to fish the dry fly. They are designed not only to keep the fly floating, but also to keep it floating as naturally as possible. For purposes of discussion, we will group these methods into two broad categories: the upstream method, and the downstream method.

FISHING THE DRY FLY

The Upstream Method

Upstream presentation is the approach used most often by today's dry fly fishermen. To some, it is the only way to fish the dry fly. Fishing in England, I was sternly informed that, regardless of where I suspected the fish to be, I

A   B   C

Fishing the Dry Fly: The Upstream Method

When fishing a dry fly upstream, be prepared for the line to start drifting back toward you the moment it touches the water. To avoid losing a fish due to such slack, you must retrieve the drifting line. First, cast (A). The moment the line hits the water, place the line you've been holding in your free hand over the index or middle finger of your rod hand (B). By pulling the line through this control point (C), the excess line can be efficiently retrieved.

must present my fly upstream of the fish. As a stately English gentleman told me, "It just isn't done any other way." As you shall learn, however, that is not necessarily the case.

True, there are several reasons, besides tradition, for using the upstream casting method. First, approaching a fish from below helps to keep us un-detected. Remember, fish face upstream into the current to better intercept their food and to facilitate breathing. Also, multiple crosscurrents exist, which create fly drag, and the upstream method helps us to reduce that problem and facilitate the natural float of the fly.

Once you have taken a position in the stream and selected the area where you wish to drop your fly, cast up and slightly across stream, allowing the fly to land above the suspected lie. As the fly begins its float downstream, retrieve, or strip in, excess line by placing the line in the index or middle finger of your rod hand and pulling with the other. That is done so that if the fish does come to your fly you can strike quickly. Keep the fly floating as long as possible, even if it has passed the spot where you thought it would be taken. Remember, after the fly enters the fish's window, the fish may follow it for some distance. This whole process may have to be repeated two and three times before the fish actually comes to the artificial fly.

Whether the cast is directly upstream, or upstream and slightly across, this technique is a tried-and-true method for fishing the dry fly. But there will be spots that can't be reached or properly fished by casting upstream, particularly in very selective spring-creeks. In such cases the downstream method may be more useful.

The Downstream Method

There will be times when a favorable presentation position cannot be obtained by upstream casting. When peculiarities of the stream flow indicate, or because of delicate water situations, such as flats, a downstream cast may be your best method. Keep in mind that your movements are now much more distinguishable to the fish. Keep your distance. Make your normal cast to a spot above the target area, but instead of retrieving line, as in the upstream uproach, feed it out at a speed that will allow the fly to float naturally. Allow the fly to float for as long as possible; the fish may follow, and you don't want to snatch the fly away from it.

Fishing the Dry Fly: The Downstream Method

As the fly line extends out on the forward cast (A), wiggle the rod quickly back and forth (B), creating serpentines in the line (C). In the water, these serpentines slowly uncoil, allowing a natural downstream float to the target. To continue the float, pay out more line.

A   B   C

FISHING THE WET FLY

The use of a wet, or subsurface, fly is the oldest method in fly fishing; it was used to the exclusion of other methods through the mid-1800s. Today, its popularity has diminished, having fallen to the more exacting science of fishing imitation nymphs.

The wet fly itself denotes a particular fly pattern designed to imitate an immature, or drowned, winged insect that has arrived from land or by water. This differs from a nymph in that the nymph, a separate aquatic stage, is not yet winged and therefore has a completely different silhouette. The two fishing methods are often referred to collectively as "fishing wet," and because the fly and the strike of the fish are not necessarily seen, but rather felt, different types of equipment and techniques are needed.

Wet flies, of course, carry more weight than the delicate dry flies. Absorbent materials tied on heavier wire hooks help the fly sink below the surface. Floating fly lines can be, and are, used for fishing wets, but the use of sink-tip and full-sinking fly lines of various densities can often help to sink a fly beyond the depths that it would reach with a floating line. Traditionally, rods used to fish wet were very soft so that they would quickly telegraph and also absorb the surprising, often jolting, strike of a fish. Today standard rods do the job well.

Once a wet fly is chosen, your first task is to determine the proper fishing depth. Remember, fish occupy places where the food comes to them. During a hatch, fish will typically locate themselves close to the surface where they can pick off the sub-aquatics as they begin to hatch, although at other times they will occupy a middle-depth position, intercepting drifting food coming off the bottom. When no hatch is in progress the fish will most often hold near the bottom of a stream where there is plenty of protection and little current. Your job, then, is to present the fly at the proper depth where the fish is located.

Quartering Down and Across

The quartering-down-and-across technique is a traditional method for fishing the wet fly. Because the line, leader, and fly, when swinging across the current, are very taut, the strike of a fish is quickly telegraphed to the angler. Also, the swinging fly appears to swim through the water, giving it a lifelike motion. For these reasons, quartering down and across is the method used most often by anglers of all abilities.

The cast is made slightly down and across stream. The current creates a belly in the line, which in turn swings the fly across the current to a final destination directly downstream of the angler. The fly is most often taken during the swing, and if it is not, the fisherman can twitch the rod, which will impart additional action to the fly.

Strikes can also occur while the fly hangs in the current below the angler, and they can be fairly abrupt. Thus, striking, or raising the rod tip to set the hook, becomes unnecessary; the fish will generally hook itself. Because fish are often hooked when the fly is in this downstream position, I have known many fishermen to forgo the cross-stream cast and swing, casting directly downstream and hanging the fly in the current. Although big fish are not often deceived by the latter method, it is the abrupt strike, so easily detected, that appeals to these fishermen.

The Across-and-Downstream-Mend Method

This method is often referred to as the grease-line or Wood's technique, (after its originator, Arthur Wood). Before the wet fly begins its swing with the current, the line is mended upstream, controlling the speed of the fly as it moves across the current. In this technique, you throw the fly slightly downstream and across. As the fly begins to swing against the current, roll an upstream mend in the line so the fly drifts at a more natural, consistent rate. You may have to mend two or three times before the fly reaches its final position downstream. Then you pick it up and repeat the process.

The Dropper Fly

The dropper fly is an old tried and true method still very effective. Based on the adage that, if one is good, two may be better, a dropper fly is simply an additional fly tied into the main leader. Some people even tie a third fly on for good measure.

The first fly is attached to the main leader tippet. About 18 inches up the leader (and this can vary), another piece of monofilament is attached and a second fly is tied to it. For those who would like to try a third fly—although I found that it creates a lot of tangling—an additional monofilament can be attached another 18 inches higher on the leader. The dropper fly technique can be fished either down and across, or down and across with a mend, depending on the current.

The wet fly is not used as frequently as the more precise nymphal imitations. Today, fishing a nymph imitation is more or less synonymous with "fishing wet." Because a nymph reacts differently in the water than any other fly, it requires different techniques to simulate its action.

A typical dropper-fly arrangement.

NYMPH FISHING

The nymph or larval stage of aquatic insects makes up the greater part of a fish's diet. As we have seen, the adult stage lasts as little as a few hours out of an insect's year-long existence, but the nymphal stage is available to the trout throughout the year, and is therefore a stage well worth imitating. The nymph has various ways of moving about in a stream, and our fishing technique must be adapted to that.

A nymph either crawls or swims near, or on, the bottom of the stream, and during hatching, it travels from bottom to surface, where it is at the mercy of the current. It is these movements that trout notice and respond to, and they can be imitated by the nymph fisherman using either downstream or upstream techniques.

Downstream and Across

This method is closely associated with fishing the wet fly but can work nicely with the nymph as well. By casting slightly down and across, the fly is allowed to swing with the current until it is directly below the fisherman. In actuality, nymphs do not swim or swing in this manner. The method works because the fly is first allowed to sink, and the current, pushing against the line, causes a rising motion of the fly, which simulates the natural upward movement of the nymph. As with the wet fly, once the fly is directly downstream, it should be held there a few seconds. The current will wave the fly in an up-and-down motion, closely imitating a swimming nymph struggling to reach the surface.

While this technique may fool some of the fish some of the time, the law of averages says that it won't fool all of the fish all of the time, and almost certainly not the largest and smartest. Yes, it is a proven technique, and with it, you will always take your share of fish. But other methods will give you better odds.

The Grease-Line-Mend Method

Here, the object is to let the nymph drift, rather than swing, with the current. This technique more closely mimics a natural nymph. Cast across and slightly downstream. As the fly sinks and begins its drift, the belly in the line must be eliminated by throwing an upstream mend, slowing the fly. An additional mend should be made as the fly moves across the current, keeping the line from interfering with the fly's natural float. The idea is to let the fly drift, instead of drag, through the water.

The Leisenring Lift

Developed by Jim Leisenring, one of the great Pennsylvania wet fly fishermen, this method takes the down and across and mend method and adds a twist.

Leisenring understood that the rising motion of the artificial nymph looks natural to the fish. As the fly, originally presented above the fish, reached the proper location, the fisherman, by lifting the rod, would impart an upward movement to the fly. This, as with other downstream methods, is particularly effective when fishing caddis pupa, which, you will remember, rise very quickly from the bottom to the surface. The technique is very simple but very effective.

Although the various downstream methods will catch an ample amount of fish, it is the upstream techniques, once learned by the angler, that, overall, will be the most productive. Cast upstream, the nymph imitation more closely resembles a natural insect.

The Continuous or Dead Drift Method

Nymphs, when they break loose from the bottom, are generally at the mercy of the current. Helpless, they must drift along until they either reach the surface for hatching, or attach themselves to another obstruction. The fisherman's challenge is to simulate this helplessness for as long as possible, and the continuous, or dead drift, method generally does the trick.

Cast the fly, quartering up and across stream. As the fly begins its downstream drift, retrieve the excess line from the water and throw an upstream mend in the line. This allows the fly to sink as deep as possible. When the fly is directly across from you, throw another upstream mend and continue mending as the fly moves downstream. The objective is to keep the fly as deep and unfettered in its drifting motion as possible. With this method, the fly will always lag to some degree, even with mending, some distance behind the fly line itself. If the fly is allowed to drift correctly, the strike will most likely occur when the fly is at its deepest point, or directly across from you.

The Direct Upstream Method

This method is far and away the most effective technique for fishing a nymph. Because you are not casting across currents which can cause drag problems, the direct upstream method allows the fly to float downstream in a natural looking dead drift manner. Cast directly upstream, above where you think fish are holding. As the fly comes toward you, strip in the excess line. If you feel or see the line stop, strike immediately by lifting the rod straight up. (More on how to strike at the end of this chapter.) When the fly is five feet away, pick it up and quickly repeat, moving six inches over from the original cast.

The Sawyer, or Skues Method

Used most on spring-creek, or slow-water, streams where the trout is seen rising or is visible to the angler, this technique is much like fishing a dry fly. Cast above the trout and allow the fly to float into the window of his vision. Remember, you are working to one fish, not a general area, so the actual drift of the fly need not be longer than 10 feet. When your fly passes the fish, cast back upstream and repeat the process.

Use of Nymph Indicators

One of the most difficult things about fishing a nymph, especially upstream, is detecting the strike of the fish. It is for this reason that many fishermen are reluctant to fish wet, preferring the dry fly, with which all the activity is observable. The downstream, or wet fly, method helps, for the strike is felt, but it is still not as effective at catching larger, warier fish as fishing the nymph upstream. What often happens is that a fish takes and rejects your fly, but because there is so much line on or in the water or the water surface is so disturbed, the strike goes undetected.

To better detect the subtle take, consider using a surface indicator. Attached to the leader 24 or 36 inches above the fly, according to the depth you wish to fish, an indicator essentially acts as a bobber. When the indicator stops or is suddenly pulled under the surface, you should immediately raise the rod, setting the hook.

Indicators take many forms. In the past, some fishermen tied a bushy dry fly (without the hook) up from the fly, but today nymph indicators, because of their acceptance by anglers, have become sophisticated. Some fly line manufacturers place at the tip of the fly line a flourescent three-foot section that can easily be seen by the angler. The butt section of some leaders are now dyed flourescent for the same reason. Acrylic yarns, stick-on foam indicators, fashioned pieces of cork, and tiny flourescent plastic tubes that can be slid to adjust for variations in depth are all highly visible, whether on or in the water, and can all be effective. Because fishermen can "see" what is happening, the use of indicators has made nymph fishing an important way of taking fish. Remember, 90 percent of a trout's feeding is done subsurface. The fisherman who is reluctant to fish subsurface is missing a big part of the sport.

Strike Indicators

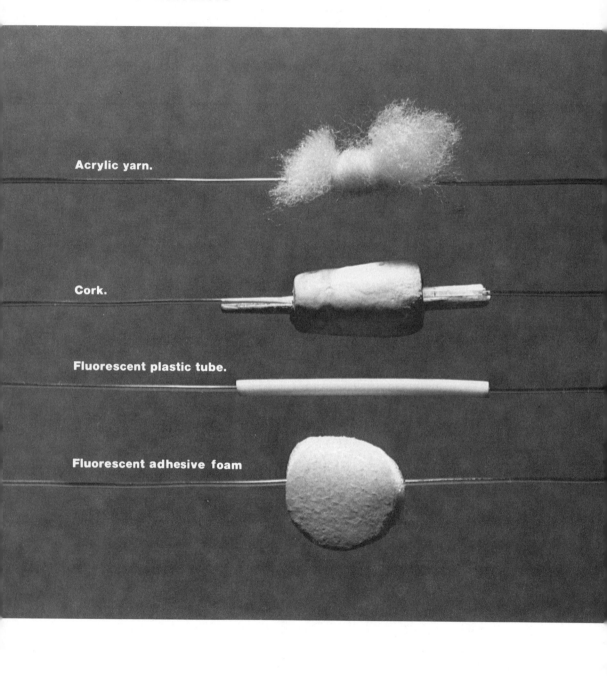

Acrylic yarn.

Cork.

Fluorescent plastic tube.

Fluorescent adhesive foam

As we have learned, once fish reach a certain size, they either supplement their diet with other fish or totally concentrate on them for their food supply. Tending to be rather lazy, big fish will expend as little energy as possible to obtain their food, looking for forage fish that are easy prey—slow-swimming, crippled, or dying.

A crippled fish has trouble retaining its momentum. Holding in one spot is a struggle. Its energy depleted, it will turn on its side and float to the surface. After regaining some of its strength it will quickly swim toward the bottom, searching for a secluded holding spot. This process will continue as the fish slowly loses ground and drifts downstream.

Oftentimes large fish will create their opportunities by swimming fiercely at a gathered group of minnows, stunning one or two, which can then be swallowed at leisure. Minnows congregate in the shallow water. When attacked, the congregation bolts out of the water, as though someone had thrown a handful of pebbles in. If you have ever seen big fish working baitfish in the ocean, you know how that looks on a larger scale.

Fishing a streamer or baitfish imitation is measured in the quality of the fish, rather than the quantity. Remember, you are now looking for larger fish, and, because their percentage of the population is small, you will have to be more persistent in your fishing.

The key to streamer fishing success is patience. In a mile section of a trout stream, perhaps less than ten percent of the fish population will feed on other fish. In addition, only two of the ten percent may have residence in the particular pool or run you have selected to cast your fly. Because big fish are known to feed only once in every three to five days, you very well may be fishing for only one or two fish within that area. For such a small, select group, you must have patience if you are to be successful.

I've known many streamer fishermen who rate the success of their days not in how many fish they have landed but in how many strikes they have had. A five- or six-strike day can be a great day, for these anglers know that, considering the size of streamer they were using, the size of fish that came to the fly very possibly would be in the trophy category. Let me illustrate. During one unusually warm fall, I fished the Yellowstone River above Livingston, Montana, and, after three full days of fishing, I could count my strikes on one hand. Discouraged, I contemplated moving to another river system, but elected to try one more run before leaving the area. On the fifth cast I hooked a beautiful six-pound German brown that made the entire three days a success. Moral: Without patience, you will never be successful in catching a trophy fish on a streamer.

Unlike fishing a nymph, where the cast and the drift are so important, fishing streamers calls for working the fly in such a manner as to mimic crippled fish. Rather than working in an upstream manner, you fish a streamer by working downstream from the head to the tail of the pool, making sure the fly is worked through all sections of the pool. There are various line retrieves and rod movements we commonly use to impart good action to the fly. Let's take a look at a few.

The Direct Left-Hand Pull

In the direct left-hand pull, you cast the fly directly across stream, at first allowing the fly to sink. As it swings across current, strip or pull the line with systematic strips and continue doing so until the fly is directly downstream from you. The strike can come at any time.

The Rod Pump Retrieve

In the rod pump retrieve, we are not retrieving line, but using the rod tip to give the streamer a darting action. After casting across stream, and as the fly begins to swing in the current, pump the rod tip sharply in an up-and-down fashion. Do so until the fly hangs in the current downstream of you. The darting action of the fly will mimic the movements of a fish that is unable to swim effectively.

The Pull-and-Pump Method

I've found the pull and pump method to be especially successful on big water where long casts are made. Because an overabundance of line is in the water, simple retrieving of the line or the pump of a rod tip will not move the fly enough to give it the telltale erratic movement of a vulnerable fish. A combination of pulling the line and pumping the rod tip simultaneously will communicate more dramatic action to the fly. Cast across and slightly downstream. As the fly begins to swing, pull down on the line held in your left hand and simultaneously pump the rod tip up and down. Allow the line to slip slowly back up through the guides, and then repeat. This is similar to the first movement of double-haul casting.

The Crippled or Panicked Retrieve

I learned the technique known as "the crippled or panicked retrieve" from one of the legendary streamer fishermen, the great writer Joe Brooks. He used it both on big water and in the shallow, placid water of spring creeks. You cast across and downstream to either a feeding fish or a selected holding spot. As the fly enters the water, flick the rod tip up and down very quickly five or six times, causing the fly to skitter just underneath the surface and creating an erratic movement that often entices big fish to strike without much hesitation. Where you know a fish is present, you will have your answer right away. Either he will move quickly to the fly or he won't. There never seems to be a middle ground. If there is no action, quickly cast to another spot.

Remember, in fishing a streamer you have to impart some erratic swimming action to the fly in order to be successful. This action will elicit the vicious strike so characteristic of big trout. If you are patient and willing to tie on the really big fly, you have as good a chance as anyone of landing the fish of a lifetime.

REVIEW

Now that you have learned a bit about equipment, how to cast the fly, where fish are likely to be, what fish are most likely to feed on, and some of the methods and techniques used to fish various fly imitations, it's time to review the step-by-step procedures required whenever we're about to fish an actual stream.

After donning your waders and rigging your rod:

1. Select a portion of the stream that will be productive, remembering the four stream types: riffles, runs, pools, and flats. Note the depth of the area and speed of the current and think about the casting, mending, and stripping techniques you'll need to fish effectively.

2. Analyze your approach, following the productive grid method of fishing a stream. Predetermine precisely where you will start fishing and where you will end, and also where you will place your first and last casts.

3. Try to determine what the fish are feeding on by first observing what insects are on the water or flying about. If no apparent feeding activity is taking place, select a general dry fly imitation such as an Adams, Royal Wulff, or Elk-Hair Caddis, and consider using a subsurface imitation—a wetfly, nymph, or streamer—if the dry fly proves to be unsuccessful.

4. After selecting the fly, determine the best method for fishing the particular imitation that duplicates the actual movements of the insect.

5. Before casting, analyze the various current problems that may disrupt your presentation and fly drift. Try to anticipate problems and take corrective measures before they happen, to avoid fly drag.

6. Now, enter the water quietly and make your first cast.

8

General Problem Solving

Regardless of their ability, fly fishermen will always be confronted with problems in catching fish. Solving those problems can often be quite frustrating, so you must develop a troubleshooting technique that at least provides a systematic method for sorting out the problems in a logical manner.

Problem solving is really a process of elimination. We observe, and then we try something; if unsuccessful, we try something else. Slowly, we eliminate all the variables, hopefully working our way to a successful conclusion. This process is much like a doctor analyzing and curing an illness. He will first observe and then eliminate all the things that could not be causing the problem. He then runs tests to determine which of the remaining possibilities is the culprit. Knowing the cause, he can implement the cure.

In fly fishing most problems fall into three categories. First is *presentation,* or where we place the fly and how it reacts while on or in the water. Second is *the fly itself.* Does it simulate what the fish is presumed to be feeding on that day or what the fish is accustomed to eating? Finally, if both presentation and fly seem correct, you must turn to *the leader.*

PRESENTATION

With presentation, the angler's concerns consist of where he is fishing the fly and how the fly is being displayed to the fish while on or in the water. Say that you have chosen a likely run of water but so far have had poor results. It's time to ask yourself a series of questions to determine if presentation is your problem. Have you covered the water systematically? Has your system been such that the fish has not been spooked? (Remember the productive grid.) Are you sure

145

Choosing the right fly, or "breaking the code" is a problem common to all anglers. But you can choose correctly if you follow a systematic approach.

of the fish's holding area? Many times I have watched a fish feed on the surface only to discover that his actual holding spot is several feet from the rise form. By casting the fly around the rise you can assure yourself that the fish has actually seen what you're offering.

Once you have covered all the productive water, and you feel confident the fish has seen your fly (with little or no result), you must then ask yourself whether the fly drifted naturally to him. Was there unnecessary fly drag? Perhaps you need to mend your line either upstream or downstream, depending on the line belly. If casting downstream, feeding line out may be all that is needed.

Generally, fly drag is quite obvious to the fisherman, but there are times when this factor will be far from clear. I remember angling over a fish during a very nice hatch, but without success. The fly imitated the hatch and, I thought, passed over the fish drag-free, but still the fish was not interested. Frustrated, I went back to the bank to consider the situation. When I reentered the water about ten feet upstream of where I had been fishing I presented the fly and on the first cast the fish gulped it down. I deduced that the problem had been a slight drag, which was discernible to the fish but not to me 30 feet away. Changing my stream position solved the problem.

Once you are convinced that the fly is being presented properly and that it has been seen by a fish, you can confidently move to the next possibility, that the fish simply doesn't like what you're dishing up.

FLY SELECTION

Selecting the right fly can be the most important and troublesome problem to the angler. Regardless of how well the fly is presented, if it is not the right one it will be rejected. In solving fly problems overall, you must first try to isolate a fly profile that the fish is feeding on or is recognizable to the fish. These basic profiles include, in the order of their elimination:

1) an upright dun or mayfly,
2) a downwinged fly of a caddis or stonefly,
3) a nymph,
4) a spinner, or spent winged fly, or
5) a terrestrial.

Yes, there are other insects of slightly different profiles, but by far these are the most common. Your next step is to determine whether you have a non-feeding or a feeding fish.

The Five Basic Profiles, in Order of Elimination

1. An upright dun, or mayfly.

2. A downwinged fly, such as a caddis or stonefly.

3. A nymph.

The Five Basic Profiles
in Order of Elimination
(Cont.)

4. A spinner, or spent winged fly.

5. Two typical terrestrials.

Selecting a Fly for Non-Feeding or Inactive Fish

Non-feeding or inactive fish are the most difficult to select flies for. Because there is no visible insect, there is no one fly you can isolate. Your procedure becomes a process of elimination, starting with an upright dun or mayfly and going through the various fly profiles until you find something of interest to the fish.

Although there is nothing sacred about it, the sequence of profile elimination should follow the progression mentioned above. Start with a conventional up-winged dry fly that most commonly imitates a mayfly dun. Next, move to a downwinged fly representing either caddis or stonefly. Moving on, try a nymph, then a spinner or spent winged fly, and finally a terrestrial type such as an ant, beetle, or grasshopper. Again, you are looking for something that is recognizable and of interest to the fish.

Getting the attention of the fish can take on many forms. Obviously, if more than one fish quickly takes your offering you can stop right there, but life is generally not that easy. It is when the fish either rises or strikes at the fly but at the last second rejects it by letting it slide on past, or jumps over it, or bats it about with his body, that you know the problem is not yet solved. Knowing that the fish at least likes something about it, your first move is to change its *size,* in most cases to a smaller fly. There will be times when a bigger fly is more acceptable, but that is not generally the case.

After you feel comfortable that you have exhausted all the size variables, you should then try the final imitation requirement, *color.* Color itself can be rather elusive, but if you have been fishing with a dark fly in various sizes with no results, try a lighter colored one. If this doesn't work, move to a different profile and start the process over again.

Selecting a Fly for a Feeding Fish

When fish are feeding, you can discard the guessing game to some extent. Observe for yourself what fly is in the air or on the water. Capturing a specimen in your hand or with a net or in your hat can help you choose a close imitation. Problems arise when two or more types of insects are prevalent.

Let's say a mayfly hatch is under way. Naturally, you select a proper profile imitation, matching both size and color. But there may be another, smaller mayfly present without your knowing it, or perhaps the fish has chosen the actual nymph as its target. Time to observe the feeding scene more closely. Also, in the midst of a mayfly hatch, a stonefly or small caddis could be depositing eggs on the water and the fish may be taking these, completely ignoring the mayfly. Such *complexed hatch situations,* as they're called, present neverending variations and problems. You must be patient. Again, eliminating the variables should lead you to the correct fly.

If you have established that the fish is seeing the fly, that the fly is floating drag-free, and that a precise imitation has been selected, you must then open your thinking to the possibility that something more mundane and not terribly obvious is your problem—namely, the leader.

LEADERS

There will always be controversy as to whether fish actually see the leader or whether the leader tippet imparts microscopic drag not apparent to the distant angler. We know that both can be a problem. Unfortunately, many good fly fishermen think the leader tippet is totally unimportant, that only presentation and fly selection need their attention. But over my many years of fishing, I have proved to myself that tippet size is often involved in one's success or lack of it. Let me illustrate.

Years ago, while fishing a famous spring creek, I had a very small mayfly hatching in profusion that eluded my every effort at imitation. The insect had a subtle yet irresistible coloration. Consequently, I concentrated my efforts on tying different hues in slightly varying styles. For about two weeks I had worked without success over three- and four-pound fish feeding on freshly hatched duns. A surprise was about to happen.

During this time a woman friend gave me some very fine transparent nylon sewing thread, which, on testing, appeared to be extremely strong. I tied a piece to the end of my leader, retied the fly, and presented the new package to the fish. Without any hesitation the fish took it. *The problem had not been the presentation or the fly, but the size of leader I was using!* I doubted that the fish had seen the leader because of my downstream casting approach, but the heavier leader was obviously setting up microscopic drag, creating an unnatural movement of the fly in the delicate-water situation. This microscopic drag was not observable to me 30 feet away, but it must have been highly visible to the fish inspecting it from one inch away.

Many people, for fear of breaking off a big fish, use leader tippets that are too large. When I hear their explanation, I emphasize to them that fish breakoff is secondary to their problem; what is primary is that the fish gets hooked in the first place. If you can't hook him, you'll never have a chance to land him.

Leaders

Smart fly fishermen always carry an assortment of leaders of different diameters with them when they go on stream.

Problem solving on the stream is an important aspect of fly fishing. It is a skill that is developed over time. The key is to be systematic, isolating and eliminating those variables that don't point to the problem. These problems can be extremely complex, taking up the better part of an entire fishing season in finding the solutions. But if you patiently adhere to an established process of elimination, concentrating first on presentation, then on the fly, then on the leader—you will almost certainly solve your problem. Moreover, you will acquire a skill that will greatly enhance a day's fishing on any body of water.

9

Hooking, Playing, and Wading Techniques

As anti-climactic as it may sound, the actual hooking and playing of fish is an important part of your fishing technique. These after-the-fact details, often completely overlooked or disregarded, pose a problem for the beginning angler.

Many factors can create the problem of an unhooked or misplayed fish, but in most cases it is *control,* or lack of it, that is at the heart of the matter. Because of inexperience, the angler finds himself unable to control or take charge of the situation before him, and the fish is either not hooked or lost in the fight. Usually, it is the fisherman's lack of *line control* that creates the problem and must be rectified if the fisherman ever hopes to land a fish.

LINE CONTROL

The system of linkages in fly fishing—fly to leader, leader to fly line—can cause difficulties for the angler. If left unattended, the line will create slack, preventing the fly fisherman either from hooking the fish or from bringing it to net. In most cases the fisherman has not established a control point from which the line can be efficiently retrieved as it floats downstream toward the angler, or efficiently fed out.

In most fly fishing techniques, the fly is presented at various angles upstream. Once upon or in the water, the line will obviously create slack as it is allowed to drift back toward the angler. If the excess line is not stripped in or picked up off the water, there is little chance that the fisherman will be able to set the hook quickly on a striking fish.

Many anglers have no such control point from which to efficiently strip in or pick up the excess line, continuing to hold the line in the hand opposite

153

The author hooks an 18-inch rainbow trout on Silver Creek. Note the position of the rod and hands: up to keep the line tight and the hook in place.

The Control Point

A   B   C

Whether fishing the fly or landing a fish, establish a control point after you cast by placing the line over the middle or index finger of the rod hand (A,B). Now excess line can be retrieved off the water and a fish can be brought to net more efficiently. When retrieving line, always pull down from below the control point (C), never from above it.

Wrong!
Never fish the fly with the line off the control point. The line can neither be paid out nor retrieved efficiently, and subduing a hooked fish with the line out of control is, at best, an awkward business.

the rod. Using an overhand method or some other unsophisticated expedient, they try to regain line as it drifts inexorably toward them. Unfortunately, slack is eliminated only in part when striking—not enough to move the fly and set the hook in the fish's jaw.

To establish the best control point after you have completed the cast, immediately place the line over the middle or index finger of the hand holding the rod. From this position you can strip in the line, not by reaching above the rod hand, but by pulling and stripping from below or behind the hand. By gently clamping down with the control finger when the fish comes to the fly, you will quickly tighten the line, creating a direct pull between you and the fish's jaw. Establishing this control point should become as automatic to you as the cast itself. Neglecting to establish it only results in frustration.

Because the finger is a highly sensitive tool, this control point can feel, through the line, what the fish is doing or what it intends to do when hooked. If the fish runs toward you, you can quickly and efficiently strip in more line; if it darts away, you can release the finger pressure, allowing the line to slip easily over the finger and out through the guides. Anglers need this sensitivity point; from it comes control, however tenuous-seeming, of the entire length of the line.

HOOKING FISH

Much can be said about how fish are hooked or, more to the point, why they are not hooked. The causes are countless but normally derive from one of five classic mistakes: (1) the angler places himself in a position too far from the fish or holding water; (2) he strikes too quickly, snatching the fly away from the fish; (3) he strikes too hard, leaving the fly in the fish's mouth; (4) he strikes too slowly; or (5) he does not strike at all.

Hooking Mistake #1: The Angler Too Far from the Fish or Holding Water

Many fishermen cast from a position much too far from the intended fish or holding lie. Unfortunately, the more line you cast, the more problems arise, especially those relating to unmanageable slack and fly drift. Also, fishing great lengths of fly line means sacrificing a certain degree of hand-eye coordination, necessary in hook-setting. Yes, there are stories of anglers making 90-foot-plus casts and hooking fish (even I have accidentally done this); but in reality, because of the amount of line involved, putting enough quick tension on the line to imbed the hook in the jaw of the fish is highly improbable. To avoid this situation, *place yourself as close to a fish or its holding water as possible or practical.* Fish as short a line as you can; you will be in better control. Remember, great lengths of line on the water, translating to unruly slack, often result in a fish not hooked.

Hooking Mistake #2:   Striking Too Quickly

Taking the fly away from a fish is another fly fishing problem, although not a common one. In very clear water it is often possible for you to watch the fish move to or follow the fly. The anticipation caused by watching the fish inspecting the fly can readily cause you to strike before it actually takes the fly, with regrettable results. When wet-fly fishing, *wait for the fish to take and turn with the fly;* when dry fly fishing, *wait for the fish to remove the fly from the surface.* Then strike.

Hooking Mistake #3:   Striking Too Hard

If you set the hook with the intention of rearranging the fish's dentures, the result will be a fly broken off the leader and imbedded in the fish's mouth. You don't need much pressure or movement to set the hook (saltwater fish excepted). Giving the rod a quick lift or snap until you feel resistance is all that you need to do. A body-and-soul jerk is almost sure to result in a lost fish and a lost fly.

Hooking Mistakes #4 and 5:   Striking Too Slow or Not Striking at All

Striking too hard is a problem, but it is striking too slow and not striking at all that are the most common mistakes, especially when fishing the dry fly. Inexperienced fishermen often become mesmerized by the fly as it drifts downstream. When the fish comes to it, the novice angler is so surprised that he stands there, rapt and motionless. For best results, anticipate the strike and try reversing the psychology. Be surprised if the fish does not take the fly, rather than if it does.

Keep your eyes on the situation at hand; inattentiveness is another cause of slow striking. The environment in which trout streams exist is often pristine and beautiful, abundant in wildlife and vegetation. There is time to enjoy these things—but not when the fly is on or in the water. If your intent is to catch fish you must devote your energies to watching what is in front of you, not what is on the bank, in the sky, or among the trees. Inevitably, the moment you let your eyes roam, the fish will decide to act. By no means am I downgrading the aesthetic aspects of the sport, for they are one of the features that make fly fishing as varied and rewarding as it is. But if the fish is to be hooked, the drama unfolding in front of you must be observed as it is happening. There are few instant replays, especially from wild, selective fish, and none in slow motion.

Many rod-setting techniques have been advocated for successful hookups. Some say, for example, that the rod needs to be taken to one side or the other, allowing the fly to seat itself in the bony corner portion of the fish's mouth. Unfortunately, I have never found one particular method to be more satisfactory than another. I advocate eliminating rod gymnastics, concentrating instead on striking with deliberate and immediate motion by raising the rod tip until pressure is felt. If the hook pulls out it pulls out. No one method can guarantee perfect results.

If the full cycle is to be completed, the fish, once hooked, must be played and brought to net. Unfortunately, playing a fish presents the angler with additional problems.

PLAYING FISH

Hooking a fish, particularly a large one, is the aspect of fly fishing that often leads to the greatest disappointment: a lost trout. The causes for such loss are many, but, once again, center on the angler's lack of control of the situation. Remember: the fly line and rod act as a telegraph, transmitting information about the fish's movements, so proper line control is an important first step in playing and landing fish. The messages from the fish's movements must be transmitted instantly to the angler, and taut line efficiently does this job. Avoid slack, not only because the fish may eject the hook, but also because slack line may not telegraph movement until it is too late.

It is difficult for a fish to spit out a fully embedded fly, regardless of slack line. To demonstrate this to fishermen, I have placed the rod on the bank and allowed a hooked fish to meander freely about his habitat. After a minute or so I again place the rod in the fisherman's hand and, to his surprise, the fish is still there. Now, I don't recommend this as a method of playing fish, for it does permit the fish unnecessary freedom to wrap the line around obstructions and break the leader. But it does illustrate that most hooked fish, left to their own devices, cannot spit that hook out.

Choosing a position within the stream to stage your fight can be crucial. Deep, fast-moving water restricts the movement of the fisherman. Therefore, I always recommend moving to shallower ground along the bank to play the fish, especially if it is decent-sized. Once there, you have more mobility to pursue the fish downstream if it is running. Also, because the bank usually has less water current, landing the fish there can be easier. Avoid the fight at center stream, for bringing a fish to net while wading in fast water puts undue strain on your terminal tackle (leader, tippet, fly), increasing the chances of the hook's pulling free or breaking off altogether.

Once the fish has been hooked, rod position is also important. The rod and tip should act much like shock absorbers, absorbing the jerking and straining of the fish, and thus protecting the more fragile leader. The rod tip should always be pointed up, or at a 45-degree angle, and should never be pointed directly at the fish. A straight pull between you and your adversary takes away an important buffer, often resulting in the separation of leader and fish. Let the fish fight the rod tip; success depends on it.

Hooking and Playing a Fish

With the exception of some downstream wet-fly techniques, the hook must be set by lifting the rod up and back when the fish is first seen or felt (A). If it is a good fish, get him on the reel and let him fight the rod as quickly as possible (B). If he wants to run, let him take line off the reel—don't strip it off yourself. And never play tug-o'-war with a big fish—he will always win.

A

B

In addition to the correct rod position, once the fish is hooked, getting the fish "on the reel" is equally important, especially if the fish is large. In most cases when a fish is first hooked, varying degrees of loose line will be hanging and dragging downstream from the angler. This loose line can become entangled and consequently a breakoff can easily occur. Reeling up excess line helps avoid this situation. If you get the fish on the reel while the fish is taking out line, the reel, with its adjustable drag, also helps to slow the fish. Use the adjustable drag that the reel provides to your advantage. Don't make the mistake of pulling out line in an effort to give the fish line or the distance from you that it so desperately seeks. Let the fish take the line off the reel: Don't do it yourself. There will be times, especially if your fish is small, when getting the fish on the reel is not necessary. Instead, you can abandon reeling up excess line and simply strip in the fish. For the most part, however, getting a fish and playing it off the reel is your best and safest approach.

A fish can respond in many different ways when hooked, but most often will make any of three basic movements: 1) It may swim away from you, 2) it may hold in the current, or 3) it may swim directly toward you. In each instance, you must respond with a different technique.

The most common direction a fish will take is *away* from the pressure of the line and rod as it is applied by the fisherman. Because novice fishermen panic or are afraid that the fish will get away, they apply far too much pressure, which all too often results in the sickening slack that tells you a leader has been broken. If the fish wants line, give the fish some line, for if you choose to play tug o' war there will be only one winner, the fish. You may have purchased the reel and line, but when the fish is hooked and running, your acquisitions instantly revert to its possession.

Apply as much pressure as you feel the leader will withstand, for your objective is to stop the run, especially if the fish has taken great quantities of line off the reel. There will be times when you will need to apply more than the normal pressure, especially when the fish is headed for heavy rapid water where you cannot follow, or snags that are certain to tangle your line. Again, apply only that amount of pressure needed to get the job done. Once the fish is stopped, then and only then do you begin recovering the lost line, either by stripping or getting it back on the reel.

When the fish swims directly toward you, the situation is reversed. Because it is not taking line from the reel, but rather creating excess line on or in the water, you must strip as quickly as possible, taking up the newly formed slack. Remember: To anticipate the fish's next movements and to remain in control of the situation, you must have a taut line. As mentioned before, a good control point is essential if the line is to be stripped in efficiently. Running up on the bank in an effort to remove slack is ineffective and dangerous.

Some fish will hold, or sulk, in the same spot and immediately go through a series of head jerks in an effort to free themselves from the pressure. Usually, this is a temporary reaction, for once the fish realizes it can't rid itself of the problem, it will choose one of the other responses, running either toward or away from the pressure. Your initial task is to keep a taut line on a sulking fish, allowing the rod tip to absorb the head jerks, and anticipate its next move. Apply as much pressure as you feel is necessary to make it do something, for constant pressure will inevitably tire the fish and enable you to bring it to net.

At one time or another all fish will perform aerial displays in their efforts to free themselves from the hook. Depending on the species, some execute these acrobatics more than others. While the fish is in the air, if the line remains tight the leader can easily be broken or the fly ripped from the mouth when the fish falls back to the surface and lands on the line itself. To eliminate this problem, adhere to the the old axiom, "bow to the jump"—that is, drop your rod tip. This movement creates a bit of slack and reduces the strain on the leader in case the fish touches down on it. Immediately after the fish reenters the water, raise the rod tip, take up the slack, if any, and proceed with the fight.

LANDING THE FISH

Perhaps the most critical point after the initial battle is when you attempt to land the fish. Up until this point, the fish has only been conscious of a relentless pressure from which it tries to get free. As it tires and swims toward the angler, it gets its first glimpse of the cause of all its problems and most often will very quickly turn tail and head away at an astonishing speed. If you are unable to release the line pressure smoothly or are unable to take your hand off the reel you will very likely be separated from the fish, permanently. Be ready for this reaction, for it may take place two and three times before the fish tires sufficiently to be netted.

In landing most reasonably-sized fish, you should always, in my opinion, use a net. Over the years, the use of nets has gone through various degrees of fashionability, but I have always found it much easier to land and handle a fish with a net than with my empty hands. It also saves time: In the confines of a net, the fish is easily controlled and hook removal is quick and clean.

First, place the net down in the water and allow the fish to slip over the rim before you raise the net out. Don't slap or reach for the fish; bring it gently

dams

Light Cahill

Gordon Quill

ght Hendrickson

Red Quill

Quigley Yellow Stone

uigley Dark Stone

Hemingway Caddis

Troth Elk Hair Caddis

oyal Wulff

Gray Wulff

Grizzly Wulff

Note: For viewing purposes, not all
es on these color pages are shown
actual size.

Humpy, or Goofus Bug

Nymph Selection

Olive Woolly Worm

Black Woolly Worm

Brown Woolly Worm

Gold-Ribbed Hare's Ear

Zug Bug

Olive Caddis Larva

Cream Caddis Pupa

Olive Caddis Pupa

Trueblood's Otter Shrimp

Prince Nymph

ve's Hopper

Letort Hopper

Black Ant

ack Flying Ant

Cinnamon Ant

Cinnamon Flying Ant

owe Beetle

ddler Minnow

Black Marabou Muddler

Matuka Light Spruce

tuka Dark Spruce

Black Woolly Bugger

Olive Woolly Bugger

Spring Creek Selection

Slate/Tan Thorax

Gray/Yellow Thorax

Gray/Yellow No Hackle

Slate/Gray No Hackle

Slate/Tan No Hackle

White/Black No Hackle

White/Black Cut-Wing Spinner

Partridge Spinner

Brown Hen Spinner

Yellow Hen Spinner

Yellow Floating Nymph

Yellow Floating Emerger

Mason Beatis Nymph

Yellow Emerger

Partridge Caddis

Whit's Black Grizzly Gerbubble Bug

Whit's Near Nuff Frog

Whit's Black and Blue

Whit's Porky's Pet

Whit's Black Water Pup

Whit's Woolly Black Leech

Olive Woolly Bugger

Whit's Chamois Leech

Whit's Crayfish

Whit's Blue Damsel

Dahlberg's Golden Diver

Hair Mouse

Salmon Fly Selection

Silver Doctor

Blue Charm

Cosseboom

Silver Rat

Rusty Rat

Black Dose

Green Highlander

Jock Scott

Salmon and Steelhead Dry Fly Selection

oyal Wulff

Gray Wulff

Brown Wulff

izzly Wulff

White Wulff

Blonde Wulff

Steelhead Wet Fly Selection

ange Fall Favorite

Skyhomish Sunrise

Bunny Black Leech

een Butt Skunk

Double Egg Sperm Fly

Saltwater Fly Selection

Dave's Salt Crab

Dave's Gray Shrimp

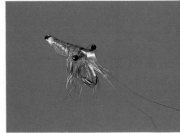

Dave's Tan Shrimp

Pearl Motivator (Bonefish)

Chico's Gold-Brown Shrimp

Pink Shrimp (Bonefish)

Dave's Salt Diver

Chico's Red/White Deceiver

Olch's Orange Glo (Tarpon)

Orange and Grizzly (Tarpon)

Olch's Squirrel Glo (Tarpon)

Chico's Yellow Deceiver

Chico's White/Blue Deceiver

Chico's White/Green Deceiver

toward you by lifting your arm and rod until it is over the net opening. Always keep the fish in the water, which absorbs the quick jerks and protects your leader. Air offers little resistance and a sudden movement may well snap the leader. Needless to say, you should never pick up a fish by the leader itself.

Striking, playing, and landing fish are the important final elements in the fishing process. Regardless of where you are when you hook a fish, you must first establish control of the situation and then anticipate what the fish will do and how the fish will do it if you are to successfully meet this final challenge. You'll learn through experience. I often think of a quotation that typifies striking, playing, and landing fish: "You have to lose a few times before you get over the fear of losing." Have faith: You'll learn from your mistakes.

Landing a Fish

When using a net to land a fish, submerge the lip of the net in the water and draw the fish over the opening (A). Never stab with the net at the fish. You will only succeed in frightening him.

Once the fish is over the opening, lift the net quickly, gathering the fish into the webbing (B).

Removing the Hook

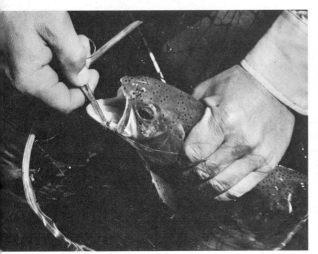

Removing the hook.
Using surgical hemostats ensures quick removal of the hook and helps prevent mutilation of both the fly and the fish's mouth.

Releasing a fish.
To release a fish after you have unhooked it, hold it firmly but gently by the belly and tail and lower it into the water, its head facing the current. If the fish is exhausted from its fight, move it gently back and forth to help pass water over its gills, giving it much needed oxygen. When it has fully revived, open your hands and let it swim free.

WADING TECHNIQUE

Wading, whether in a small creek, a lake, or a big river system, is an important aspect of fishing. Since rivers come in a variety of sizes, to reach the many places where fish reside often requires some type of wading. Fishing from the bank limits the amount of water that you can cover. Therefore, you must get into the water, in a manner both safe and easy.

   If you move through the water like a herd of elephants, you are likely either to slip or to scare fish. Both are counterproductive. Your wading technique should be aimed at safety and minimal water disturbance. Good wading style should emphasize slow, shuffling, probing movements, allowing you to feel any potential problems in your path. Walking in a stream as if it were a city street will prevent you from detecting hazardous changes in the slippery, uneven bottoms that all rivers possess. Although wading techniques should remain the same whether you are in slow, non-current water or in fast-moving, freestone streams, each water type presents special troubles that must be of concern to you.

Wading.
Wading through the water like a stampeding bull (left) only serves to put fish down. For better angling results, wade carefully and quietly (right).

Slow or current-free waters, such as spring creeks or lakes, can be deceptive. Knock-you-down current may not be present, but the very calmness of the water means that your movements can easily be transmitted to the fish. Thus, small, shuffling movements, rather than high knee steps, are imperative. Current-free water usually has a fairly even, non-rocky bottom, but perils can still be present, particularly mud. I know many a fisherman who avoids this type of water, for sinking in what appears to be bottomless mud can create some very tense and dangerous situations.

When wading in mud always make sure that one foot is on a solid bottom before venturing another step forward; if the mud becomes bottomless you can easily backtrack. In most cases, you'll find bottom, but, even so, always probe first, since getting mired in the mud can be troublesome. Once your feet become imprisoned, your next attempted step can easily produce a face-first fall into the water. If you get seriously stuck, try to free one foot at a time.

Spring creeks and lakes are not always the easiest places to wade, but it is freestone streams or fast-current waters that bring forth the greatest intimidation to many anglers. This type of streambed is primarily made up of rocks of various sizes and shapes, which can trip you and, because of the nutrient content of the water, can be very, very slippery. To minimize these wading dangers, it's important again to probe and feel your way across the stream.

When entering fast water, always stay parallel to the current; if you turn

Crossing a River

The best place to cross a river is at the tail portion of a run or a pool (foreground). The angler in the background has chosen to cross in the fastest water and is undoubtedly headed for disaster (A).

perpendicular to the current, it has greater surface area to push against and can easily throw you off balance. Before taking a step, be sure that your upstream foot is firmly planted and secure; then, and only then, shuffle and probe with your downstream foot for any obstacles. Once you have located solid footing, you can move your anchor foot forward.

The length of each of your steps is also important; they are not the same length. I call the proper movement the one-and-a-half step shuffle. As it probes, the downstream foot can take a full step more easily than can the upstream foot. Because the current is pushing hard on the upstream leg, it should move only far enough to meet the other foot. Avoid walking as you normally would, one step in front of the other, and *do not probe with the upstream foot;* the current pushing on your upstream leg can sweep it down and underneath you, quickly knocking you off your feet.

Crossing a fast-moving stream requires foresight. Always try to cross at the tail end of runs or pools where the stream is shallow and has a diminished current. Avoid heavy riffles, for these areas will inevitably get you wet. Also, when crossing it is best to angle downstream; in other words, go with the current, not against it. Finally, don't look directly down at your feet; keep your gaze five to ten feet beyond your movement. Looking directly down at the rushing water can create a sensation of vertigo, which often results in loss of balance. Let your feet be your eyes.

Crossing is always easier if you angle downstream, rather than at right angles to the current (B). Go with the current. Don't fight it.

Wading Staffs and Other Wading Aids

Aside from knowing how to step and where to cross, you can obtain devices to help you move about safely in the water.

A wading staff is an indispensable appendage for some fishermen, offering additional balance in fast water. Wading staffs can be useful, and certainly the older we get the more we depend on them. They can be purchased (in various collapsable lengths) or found on the bank in the form of tree limbs. Regardless of what type you select, always plant it on the *upstream* side of your body before taking your step. Placing the staff downstream offers nothing to lean against while you are probing with the downstream foot.

As good and useful as staffs are, they can present problems when not in use. Attached to the angler by a cord, most are allowed to drag downstream when not in use. Unfortunately, excess fly line also drifts downstream and can get caught on the dragging staff while you are in the process of either casting or retrieving. That complicates your movements and can result in the loss of fish. Although I have never found an ideal solution to this problem, I can only advise that keeping the excess line between you and the staff as short as possible will help.

The buddy system is another aid when you cross a stream. Cross arms with a companion by placing your hands on one another's shoulders for leverage. In that manner, each of you supports the progress of the other across the

Wading Staffs

A wading staff can provide you with additional balance in fast water.

Wading staffs can be made of wood (left) or metal (right).

Some metal models can be folded for easy storage.

stream, compensating for one another's balance problems and mistakes. I like
this technique not only because of its security but also because it is often the
fastest way to get across a stream.

Inevitably, you will get yourself into a position where you have either
waded too deep or, to get into a better position for landing a fish, need to
backtrack to shallower ground. This move can be accomplished in two ways:
1) by stepping backwards, or 2) by pivoting and then walking forward, toward
the bank. In stepping backward, use the same technique as you used in moving
forward. Plant your upstream foot firmly and use your downstream foot to
probe and feel for the bottom. Again, a one-and-a-half step progression is best.
If you wish to change direction completely, first "pivot" on the downstream
foot, allowing your upstream leg to drift with the current until it has found solid
footing. Try not to pivot on the upstream foot, which places your body perpendicular to the force of the water, potentially causing trouble.

At one time or another if you fish a great deal, you are sure to slip and
go down in a wading situation. It's almost as inevitable as death and taxes. In
99 percent of the cases, the worst that will happen is that you'll get wet, which
in itself can be a rather chilling experience. But there are times, especially when
you wade in deep water, that some trouble can occur. The secret is not to panic,
for in most cases you are within a few steps of finding solid ground. If your
waders fill up in deep water paddle your feet toward the solid ground. If you
are swept away by the current don't fight it, but rather let the current drift you
to quieter, less swift water, where you can stand up.

Good wading technique is logical. Know where you're wading; look for
any visible problems on the bottom; and probe and feel your way across the
stream. Wading is not dangerous; in most cases the worst that can happen is
that you will spend time drying your clothes. If you keep your wits about you
and don't rush as you wade, your fishing should be both secure and enjoyable.

10

Spring Creek Fishing

Spring creeks, or flat, slow-moving waters, present the most difficult and challenging fishing situations for all fly fishermen. Because of the complex insect populations, the very slow, gin-clear water, and the often highly sophisticated, selective fish, many anglers avoid spring creeks altogether. I have seen many fishermen commence the cocktail hour at eleven in the morning, rather than the traditional five in the afternoon, after becoming mystified to the point of despair by the complex hatch and feeding activity characteristic of this water. Still, spring creeks offer large fish and tremendous challenges, and for both these reasons, they are the classic fly fishing waters.

"Spring creek" is a generic term describing a type of water known in England as a "chalk stream," and in the eastern United States as "limestone waters." Because the creeks' main source of water is underground, water temperatures remain constant, creating an ideal environment for both aquatic insects and fish. Also, the large underground aquifers that feed spring creeks contain a great deal of the limesalts that create high alkalinity, so important to stream life. Huge weed and grassbeds flourish, which, in turn, harbor great populations of insects and offer protection for fish. Compared to streams of more normal alkalinity, the creeks' insect populations are enormous, in terms of types of species as well as in sheer numbers. Spring creeks are literally insect factories in which the resident fish grow to be both large and selective in their feeding habits.

There are additional factors that give spring creeks a special mystique. Though in places they may resemble freestone streams, with pockets, pools, and runs, for the most part spring creeks consist of flat, slow-moving water. Because the water moves at a snail's pace, fish have ample time to examine your offering, determining whether the fly adheres to the fish's present feeding interests. If it

169

With their gin-clear waters and complex insect hatches, spring creeks present perhaps the greatest angling challenge to fly fishermen.

doesn't, you don't catch fish. Your fly, therefore, must be a more exacting imitation than is needed on other types of water.

Finally, fish tend to lie fairly close to the surface when surface-feeding in spring creeks. In these instances, the cone-shaped window through which the trout views its food is quite small, maybe only four to six inches in diameter, and the fly must be presented precisely where it will float over the fish, thus adding to the angler's problems.

The quality of a spring creek is not necessarily measured by the quantity of fish you catch; it has more to do with the fascination of meeting a challenge with your wits and skill. Even though spring creeks are difficult to fish, the problems encountered can be overcome as long as you approach them intelligently and systematically. You must understand insect hatches and present the appropriate fly selections.

HATCHES AND FLY SELECTION

Spring creeks offer a buffet of food for fish. Other than the apparent mayflies, caddisflies, and small midges, they harbor good populations of damsel and dragonflies as well. Crustaceans, such as fresh-water shrimp, crayfish, sowbugs, backswimmers, and the like, add still another dimension to the smorgasbord. Moreover, each stage of each species represents a different kind of feeding opportunity that the fisherman must be aware of. A basic understanding of entomology is essential.

As I have mentioned, slow-moving water necessitates a more precise selection of fly imitation. The size, profile, and color of the fly need to be exact; they should not be compromised if you can help it. Since the flies must be tied with such precision, the use of hackle, or the wrap feather that gives our conventional dry fly patterns such a fuzzy appearance, must be kept to a minimum or in some cases avoided. Body and wing outline are extremely important on flies used for spring creek fishing, and hackle can distort the profile of the fly. Fly-pattern styles such as compara dun, thorax types, and parachute flies (where the hackle is tied horizontal to the hook, versus perpendicular), work well. But it is the no-hackle flies, popularized by Doug Swisher and Carl Richards, that in my opinion are the most effective types used on spring creeks today.

The following is a fairly complete list of fly patterns that will duplicate most fly hatches on spring creeks throughout the United States and various parts of the world. Many hatches are similar in coloration but different in size; I have listed the basic color patterns. If purchased in a variety of sizes, these flies should meet the various spring-creek fishing criteria. Note also: Two basic

Some spring creek hatches are so dense, that the chance of a trout taking your imitation are nearly impossible. In this photograph, a cloud of Tricorythodes, or "trico," as they are commonly known, has reached the spinner stage and is about to hit the water.

Because spring creek water is so clear and the food so abundant, fly imitations must be more exact than for most other fly fishing situations. There is a trico imitation in this picture. Can you find it?

fly styles are listed, no-hackles and thorax type, for the purpose of availability. Depending on where you do your fishing, one or both styles should be available. Remember, local assistance is invaluable.

Spring Creek Fly Assortment

Gray/Yellow No Hackle, #16, #18, #20, #22
Slate/Tan No Hackle, #14, #16, #18
Slate/Gray No Hackle, #16, #18
White/Black No Hackle, #20, #22, #24
Brown Henspinner, #14, #16, #18, #20, #22, #24
Yellow Henspinner, #16, #18
White/Black Spinner, #20, #22, #24
Pale Morning Dun Emerger, #16, #18, #20, #22
Gray Thorax, #14, #16, #18
Olive Thorax, #16, #18, #20
Pale Morning Dun Floating Emerger, #16, #18
Pale Morning Dun Floating Nymph, #18
Brown Ephemerella Nymph, #12, #14, #16, #18
Mason Beatis Nymph, #16, #18
Partridge Caddis, #14, #16, #18, #20

Precise fly imitations are needed, but good fishing approach is equally important.

FISHING APPROACH

The approach to spring creek fish is much like a safecracker's approach to a safe. You must be delicate and careful, moving slowly, and closely observing the situation in front of you. Because spring creek water is not "readable" in the sense of riffles, runs, and pools, you generally locate fish by looking for feeding activity. Spring-creek fishing thus becomes a hunting and stalking operation, where you spot the prey and then make your stalk to take it. Pick one fish and move very carefully toward it, for disturbances in this water will not only cause it to stop feeding but can "put him down" (off feeding) for the remainder of the hatch. Wading through the water as though you were late for dinner will only spell disaster. Once you know the fish's whereabouts, you must maneuver into a position to cast to it.

Traditionally, it has been thought that the upstream cast is solely associated with fishing the dry fly, regardless of what type of water you are on. It's true that in fast water, upstream casting helps minimize fly drag and places the angler below the fish's area of perception, but in spring creeks the conventional upstream cast is likely to be unsuccessful. Why? Because the first thing the trout views of this cast is not the fly, but the leader. What to do? By maneuvering himself upstream and at a 45-degree angle to the fish, the trouter can present the fly and allow it to drift *downstream,* ahead of the leader, making it more acceptable to the trout. Whether or not the fish actually sees the leader remains a topic of controversy, but we do know that presenting the fly in this manner is far more effective than the conventional upstream approach. Remember: *fly first, not leader first.*

Before making your cast, stand for a moment and watch the feeding characteristics of the fish. Some fish will hold and feed in one position, while others will move from side to side and/or upstream and down. Look for the fish's feeding pattern and present your fly accordingly. If you don't and the fish is rather active in its feeding movements, a mispresented fly can be trouble. Let me give you an example.

Fishing with a customer one day, I approached a very large rainbow feeding on small mayfly spinners in a very shallow backwater where the current was nonexistent. The fish's feeding pattern was distinctive. It would start at one end of the backwater and slowly make its way upstream, sipping the small naturals as it went along. Upon reaching a certain spot, it would turn downstream, swim back to its original starting position, and repeat the process. Knowing that in the shallow clear water a poorly laid cast would be detected during the fish's upstream movement, we waited until it turned away from us and headed for its starting position before we made our cast. On our fourth presentation, the fish made the mistake of taking our offering instead of a natural. The fish would never have been hooked if we had not first watched and analyzed the situation before casting.

CASTING ON SPRING CREEKS

In spring creeks, there are a multitude of current changes, most caused by the weedbeds abundant in these waters. Since the drift of the fly is crucial, and since several different currents can exist between you and the fish, you need to present your fly in such a manner as to produce slack in both line and leader so that the fly itself is not affected by these extraneous water movements. Remember, you are fishing to one fish, not an entire holding area; therefore, the float of the fly must be absolutely natural, covering not more than ten feet.

Fly casts that create slack line go by many names—the pile cast and the hesitation cast, to name two—but they all have the same goal: to pile the leader on the water surface so that while the fly journeys downstream to the fish the leader unravels quietly, creating a natural float. To create this slack while casting, stop the rod abruptly at the end of the forward cast (11 o'clock). This causes the line and leader to bounce back much like an elastic band, and the leader to fall to the water in serpentines, or on top of itself.

Because the amount of coiled leader can vary from cast to cast, and because the fly should be kept from dragging before it reaches the fish, you must also feed out additional line as the fly makes its way downstream. To do this, quickly flip the rod tip up, which will propel the line through the guides and out onto the water. Feeding line must be done before the drifting fly runs out of coiled leader. Therefore, as soon as the fly begins its drift, start feeding more line.

Your overall intent should be to place the fly in a direct line above the fish, but even the most expert of anglers sometimes miscast. Fortunately, however, we can maneuver the fly into the proper position. In many cases, fly casts are too long, going beyond our target area. To bring the fly into proper alignment to the fish, all you have to do is lift the rod tip very slowly, and actually drag the fly into position. Once it's where you want it to be, quickly drop the rod

A   B   C

Fishing a Spring Creek

Spring-creek fishing is really a hunting, stalking, and, often-times, a waiting game. After isolating a feeding trout, quietly maneuver yourself upstream of it so that it is in a quartered down-stream position (at a 45-degree angle) to yourself, and plan on casting to a target four to eight feet above it (A).

Make your cast, stopping the for-ward part of the movement at the eleven o'clock position (B). This causes the line and fly to jerk back, creating slack for the fly's drift to the fish.

After the forward cast touches down, keep the rod tip high (C). Then . . .

tip and begin feeding line out until the fly reaches the fish. Not only does this technique eliminate visible coiled leader around the fly, it also realigns the fly for the proper drift line to the fish, which is equally important.

What I have discussed is the *basic* approach to presenting a fly to a fish on a spring creek. So that it becomes perfectly clear, let's review in sequence the necessary steps for fishing success.

Assuming that, by observation, including netting or scooping insects, you have chosen a fly that meets precisely the requirements of size, profile, and color:

1) Select one fish worthy of your efforts.

2) Carefully and quietly maneuver into a position where the fish is at a 45-degree angle downstream of you.

3) Watch the fish's feeding habits, determining whether it is moving about or is stationary.

4) Pick a spot where you wish the fly to land above the fish.

D

E

F

. . . very quickly drop the rod tip down, almost to the water's surface (D). This piles additional line on the surface, ensuring the fly's continuous, drag-free drift to the fish.

You can also feed out more line for a drag-free drift by shaking the rod tip up and down, or from side to side (E). Never let the water current pull out additional line; that can only lead to drag.

If the cast goes beyond the intended target, very slowly lift the rod tip and carefully drag the fly to the proper position (F). Now quickly drop the rod tip, feeding out line *before* the fly reaches the fish's window.

5) Make your cast, but stop it abruptly at 11 o'clock on the forward cast, causing leader to pile up on the surface.

6) If the cast is too long, lift the rod tip, slowly dragging the fly into position.

7) As the fly begins to drift toward the fish, feed line out by quickly flipping the rod tip.

8) If the fly is not taken, allow it to drift downstream beyond the fish before picking up and recasting.

Once again, remember, *you are fishing to one particular fish.* The fly's float distance is no more than eight or ten feet, with the fly first presented five to six feet above the fish and allowed to float on another four feet or so beyond him before it is removed from the water and recast. Strive for as little water disturbance as possible. Also, don't give up on the fish after only one or two casts. If you have selected the right pattern, if you have made the proper presentation and drift, and, if you are persistent, you will be successful.

Successfully deceiving a selective trout in a spring creek is one of fly fishing's greatest satisfactions.

NOTES ON SPRING CREEK EQUIPMENT

Spring creeks dictate a bit more thought on equipment needs than one would use on the average river, a requirement sometimes overlooked even by accomplished anglers. In general, spring creek rods, reels, and leaders are more delicate and precise.

The emphasis placed in choosing the average fly rod is on fly casting, with little attention given to its fishability. Since flat-water leader tippets are very fine, ranging from 5x to 7x in diameter, your spring creek rod should be relatively soft so that it can absorb the strike and run that large fish make on these gossamer leaders. In addition, fly line should be chosen not only to match the soft rod's flex but also to minimize unnecessary water disturbance when it lands. Fly line should be within the three- to six-weight category. Heavier weight lines are totally unnecessary and often detrimental to your fishing. Finally, because the leader tippets used are so delicate, a smooth-running reel with a fine adjustable drag helps to protect from breakoffs.

The quality of spring creek fishing is not necessarily measured in the quantity of fish you catch; it has more to do with the fascination of meeting its special challenge with your wits and skill. I can tell you that the challenge is great and the rewards even greater. They represent the classic in dry fly fishing and may very well be the ultimate in the sport.

11

Fly Fishing Lakes and Ponds

Many people think of fly fishing as restricted solely to streams and rivers. But because lakes and ponds offer quantity, variety, and many times very large fish, including trout, they present fishermen with fine opportunities to expand their angling experience. Consequently, lakes should be on the must-do list of any fly angler.

There is something mysterious about a lake. What lurks in its depths is a question that excites the imagination. Sinking a fly through the lake's various strata, retrieving it, and feeling the unexpected strike of a fish, I come to realize that fishing a lake can never be boring: the allure of the unknown is always there.

To fish lakes successfully, you must understand their aquatics, structure, and depth. Because lakes are different from streams, featuring a distinct aquatic environment, you must also alter your fishing technique, equipment, and angling thought.

AQUATIC LIFE

Conventionally, lakes are divided into two categories, highland and lowland types. The differences in elevation mean differences in both the types and the quantity of food in them. Lowland lakes, up to 6,000 feet, are generally the most fertile, containing the greatest array of aquatic food sources for fish. Higher in altitude, especially above 10,000 feet, aquatic life dramatically diminishes and becomes very specific to the region.

With their insect diversity, lowland lakes are often more productive than high lakes in terms both of numbers and size of fish. Often, immense popula-

Don't restrict your angling to streams and rivers. Good trout can also be taken on cold-water lakes and ponds.

tions of insects are fed upon by the fish during all stages of their development, offering a smorgasbord of food for fish. In addition, leeches, various crustaceans including freshwater shrimp, and, of course, other fish further enhance the diet. Although the mayfly and caddisfly are found in all types of waters, including lakes, there is a host of food types in the lake's ecosystem that can be preferable to the fish. Slow-water species, such as midges, damselflies, dragonflies, leeches, and shrimps, are some of these.

Midges are one of the most important contributors to the food chain in both lowland and highland lakes. In fact, where waters are very cold, the midge may be the predominant aquatic insect. That is certainly the case in cold regions such as northern Canada. Fish eat all the various midge stages, from larva to adult; therefore, if you intend to fish Northern lakes, you need to carry representative patterns.

Damsel and dragonflies are among the more significant insects on lakes and ponds. Most of the time these flies are fished imitating their sub-aquatic, or nymphal, form—the adult stage of these insects is not often available to the fish, which makes a surface, or adult, imitation unnecessary.

Leeches and crustaceans are also greatly prized by lake fish. Leeches are universal, and, because of their quantity, fish feed on them readily. In addition, freshwater shrimp (crustaceans) are an important and common food source. In some lowland lakes, it is not unusual to find populations of 200 to 500 freshwater shrimp per square foot. Anglers should carry several patterns to imitate each of these food sources.

The above insects and crustaceans tend to be the primary food sources in lakes and ponds, but they are certainly not the only edibles available. Very large fish have very big appetites, and forage, or baitfish, are the most obvious way to satisfy their needs. Consequently, if trophy-size trout are your objective, fishing various streamer imitations is often a good bet, regardless of the lake's altitude.

As you move higher into the mountains, insect diversity diminishes, making fishing frightfully difficult or sinfully easy. Only one or two specific insects may be present, and exacting fly imitations are often needed to seduce the selective trout. The opposite can also be true: Anything that falls to the water may quickly be devoured by the undernourished fish population. In general, observe what is on or in the water for a clue to local feeding. Shoreline debris is also a source of information. High lakes can be fickle, but, because of the location, are a delight to fish.

Primary Foods for Lake and Pond Fish, Plus Their Representative Imitations

Midges.

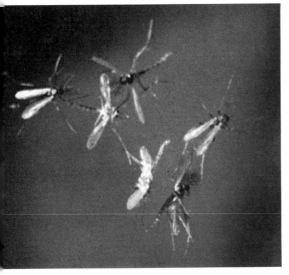

Midge imitation.

Damselfly nymph.

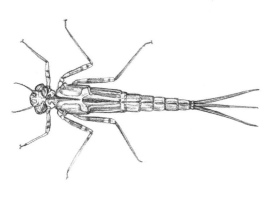

Damselfly nymph imitation.

Primary Foods for Lake and Pond Fish, Plus Their Representative Imitations (Cont.)

Leech.

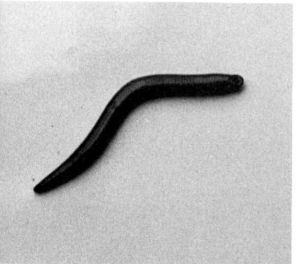

Leech imitation.

Shrimp.

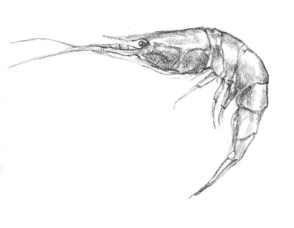

Shrimp imitation.

Food sources are important, but, as on all fishing waters, if you don't know where to place your fly, you may be the world's greatest entomologist and still fail.

At first glance, lakes and ponds give very few clues as to the whereabouts of the fish. Unless fish are actually rising, the smooth, expansive surface serves to conceal the underwater topography, making the entire impoundment appear to be a vast, unreadable wasteland. Streams are made of runs, pools, riffles, and flats, all of which say something definite about fish lies. To the inexperienced fisherman, lakes do not have these obvious signs. Yet they do have other characteristics that can actually be read as easily as a stream. Let's look at a few of the more distinguishable places in which fish will be located.

Inlets and Outlets

Drainage lakes are by far the most productive and also the most abundant of the stillwater fisheries. Water inlets arrive from streams, providing plentiful spawning areas, additional food supplies, and fresh oxygen. Therefore, inlets and outlets, if present, are among the first areas you should fish in an impoundment. Fish congregate around these spots, and they should be fished extensively.

Weed Beds

In lowland lakes weedbeds are very important. As altitude increases, weedbeds thin out. In the very high lakes they are often nonexistent. As you might suspect, weeds harbor aquatic insect life, and fish like to be close to their food sources. When fishing weedbeds, place your fly on the edges, holes, or channels of the beds, making it more visible to the fish.

Drop-Offs

Just as in streams, fish have a natural liking for depth changes, often referred to by bass fishermen as "structure." Where the geomorphology of the lake is altered there is an ideal place for fish—and for the fisherman to place his fly.

In shallow lakes, drop-offs are easily spotted. But in deep water there are some anglers, especially the bass fishermen, who use sonar depth finding equipment that aid the fisherman in discovering the underwater structure. Although I am not a confirmed advocate, these instruments not only map the lake bottom but locate schools of fish as well, which does help explain some questions about fish location.

Another classic drop-off situation is the location of the old streambed if the lake is manmade. Fish will always hold in these areas.

Islands

Small islands are another important area near which fish will hold. Aquatic insects congregate in the shallows, thus providing an irresistible food source for the fish.

Points of Land

Where land protrudes into the lake, fish will congregate. A point of land is actually a depth change. A point does not stop at the bank but extends under the water for some distance, making for a depth change situation on either side of the point. Fish that reside near jutting points of land enjoy the advantage of both depth and any food supplies migrating to these areas.

Snags and Deadfalls

Deadfalls are found in all lakes but are extremely important in high mountain lakes. They provide overhead protection for cruising trout and harbor-clinging aquatic insects. I think I've never visited a high lake where I didn't find one or two fish hanging around shoreline deadfalls. Deadfalls can be a nuisance for fishermen because of snagging, but don't pass them up.

Coves

Coves are generally the shallowest places in lakes and invariably have the warmest water. In the early part of the season fish will congregate in coves because they are among the first places insect activity will be found. Throughout the season, I always look for rising, feeding fish in these areas, for as a rule, fish cruise through coves looking for easy prey.

Underground Springs

Springheads are extremely important to all stillwater fisheries, especially if they are the main source of a lake's or pond's water. The constant temperature and fresh oxygen supplied by the underground water help provide an ideal environ-

Reading a Lake

Typical holding areas for trout in a lake include, clockwise, top, snags and deadfalls, weedbeds, islands, points of land, coves, (including dropoffs and springheads), and inlets or outlets. Studying the topography around a lake can yield further clues concerning trout whereabouts.

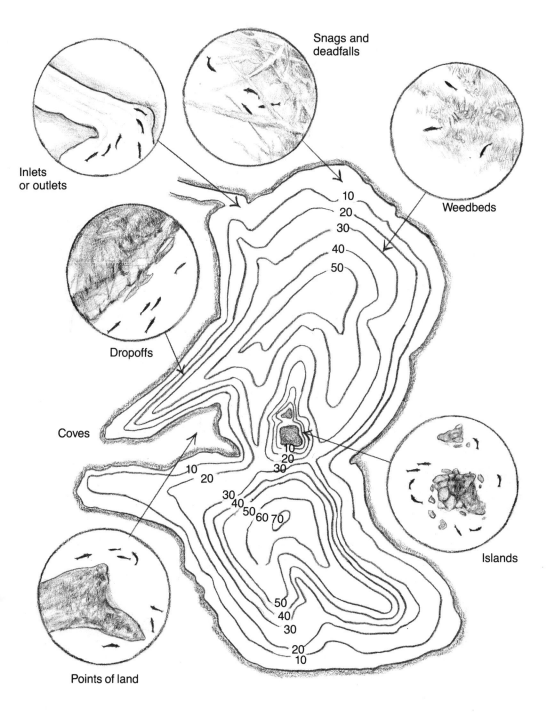

Snags and deadfalls

Inlets or outlets

Weedbeds

Dropoffs

Coves

Islands

Points of land

ment for fish. But because they are subsurface, springs are often difficult for fishermen to locate. Listening to other anglers who may have stumbled onto a spring is always a good way to get information. Bubbles coming to the surface are another indicator of an underground water source. Also, because spring sources deposit white calcium in the area of the springhead, there will be distinguishing white marks nearby. You can also take temperature readings. General lake water is 60 to 65 degrees; a spring will be closer to the 50-degree mark or colder.

A good rule to follow is this: If you find a spring, fish the area hard.

Cliffs and Rock Faces

Cliffs and rock faces are generally the deepest shoreline parts of lakes and ponds. The crevices in the rocks harbor both insects and baitfish, so that fish of all sizes cruise these areas. The shadows shed by the rock and outcroppings along its face also provide shelter available nowhere else in the lake. You should always fish near these outcroppings.

Land Topography

There will be times when the lake or pond will show no inlets or outlets, snags, points of land, islands, or visible drop-offs. What do you do then? *Look to the land around the lake,* for it might give you clues as to what is happening underwater.

Visualize the continuation of whatever landmarks there are extending under the water from the lake's shoreline. Draws and undulations at the lake's edge are indicators of possible underwater drop-offs. These might be your best clue to where the fish will lie. In general, *try to visualize the lake in cross-section.*

Feeding Fish

It may sound odd even to mention that if you find surface feeding fish you should cast your fly to them, but for some reason I have seen countless fishermen ignore this obvious sign and pursue other kinds of areas. Don't miss your chance. The fish are solving a very important problem for you: location. There is no need to guess.

The areas discussed above are not the only ones fish will hold in lakes, but they are the prominent ones. Now that you have a better idea of the fishable topography of a lake, you need to address another important factor, the depth at which fish hold.

FISHING DEPTH

The ecosystem of a lake can be complex. The productivity of a lake is measured in terms of its ability to retain oxygen, its layering of solar energy for photosynthesis, and its temperature ranges.

Like all creatures, fish seek the most comfortable place or depth to reside, where they will have the most advantageous mix of the elements that are vital to their survival.

Lakes have three layers that are significant in understanding where fish will be: the *epilimnion,* the *thermocline,* and the *hypolimnion.* The top layer, the epilimnion, can be as little as a few inches, extending down to as much as 60 feet. Because the water temperature in this layer is generally too warm for comfort, fish will not reside here. The middle layer, the thermocline, is the stratum most fish seek. Beginning anywhere from a few inches to the rare depth of 60 feet below the surface, the thermocline is generally only three to ten feet thick but contains the optimum combination of oxygen, temperature, and light penetration. The bottom layer, or hypolimnion, may be quite thin, only a few inches up from the bottom, or thick, extending upward to meet the more ideal level of the thermocline. Regardless of thickness, though, the hypolimnion is unlikely to hold fish because of a lack of oxygen and unsuitable temperatures.

It should now be obvious that, in addition to understanding the most likely physical habitats for fish, you need to discover the depth at which the fish are concentrated. To ignore the layering aspect of the lake environment is to limit your degree of success. When you fish a lake your main objective is to place yourself where the fish are. The fish are there and if you can find the spot, you will catch them.

LAKE FISHING TECHNIQUE

The feeding habits of lake fish can lend themselves to either surface or subsurface fishing. There are times for both, and it is up to the angler to analyze what is happening and use the appropriate method based upon the situation.

Dry fly or surface fishing is obviously appropriate when the fish are feeding on adult insects in or on the surface film. Because there is no current, the fish swims to the fly, rather than waiting for the fly to drift to it. Therefore, after selecting an appropriate imitation, you must determine the direction the fish is moving and make your cast ahead of it, leading it slightly. If you cast directly at a rise form, you stand the chance of either spooking the fish or placing the fly where the fish was, not where it is going. Watch for dorsal and tail fins to indicate direction.

You'll need a floating fly line, and the dry fly you select is just as important as when you are fishing rivers and streams. Analyze what is on the water and make your choice using the same imitation requirements you always use—size, profile, and color.

Fishing the dry fly is fun and exciting, but to most serious lake fishermen, fishing the underwater stage of the insects and other life forms is not only the most important but also the most productive method. It is often said that 90 percent of feeding in a stream is done beneath the water's surface. In a lake the figure may be closer to 98 percent. I have even seen anglers who know this fooled into thinking that the fish were surface feeding when in actuality they were feeding on nymphs just below the surface. What happens is that the upward momentum of a fish chasing down its prey creates the apparent rise form that is typical of surface feeding. Fishing subsurface imitations is so prevalent in lakes and ponds that even I, a professional fisherman, have trouble remembering the times when I have actually used a dry fly.

Nymph or Subsurface Technique

In using a subaquatic imitation (except in shallow lakes or for near surface-feeding fish), you must first change your fly line from a floating to a sinking type, tie on the appropriate nymph or subsurface imitation, and then try to determine at what depth the fish are feeding, or where the thermocline layer is located. To do this, sink and retrieve the fly at various depths until some action or response by the fish occurs. Either start at the surface and work down, or vice versa. Employ a counting method ("One thousand one, one thousand two," etc.) to identify the proper depth for future casts.

Ideally, you want line, leader, and fly to sink at the same rate, but that seldom happens. The leader is not of the same density and therefore lags behind the sink rate of the fly line. To counter this problem your flies should be weighted, allowing at least the fly and fly line to sink at the same rate. To further remedy the leader problem, use very short leaders, no more than three to six feet in length.

Once the fly has reached the desired depth, it is time to retrieve the line, mimicking the swimming motion of natural insects or fish. With the rod tip *extended downward, into the water,* first make one or two long retrieves, or pulls, of the line, making sure, as you do so, to press it against the rod handle with the middle or index finger of your rod hand. These first long strips will straighten out most of the irregularities that might have developed in the line, leader, and fly during their descent. After you straighten the line, your retrieves

The Figure-8, or Overhand Retrieve

This is a useful slow retrieve when fishing nymphs in either lakes or streams. Use the thumb and finger (A), to gather line in the palm of the hand (B). Repeat the maneuver by dipping and lifting the hand for more line (C). Once you've gathered four or five coils (D), drop them to avoid tangles and continue the retrieve.

This popular finger retrieve should be used with caution since removing the line from the fingers can be difficult, and in salt-water fishing, where the fish can be large and powerful, the angler risks injuring or even losing a finger if there's a strike.

A

B

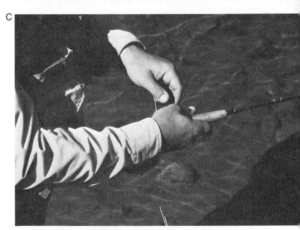

C

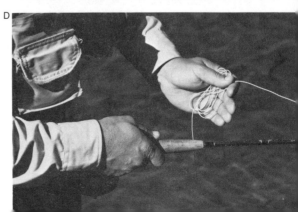

D

should follow one of several patterns designed to make the fly mimic natural movements.

The most common retrieve is rhythmic: a series of even-length pulls that make the fly swim or dart like a lively insect. Another popular retrieve is to strip the fly five or six times and then stop, which lets the fly settle as insects often do. To make the fly swim slowly, rather than dart, there is also the overhand, or figure eight, retrieve where the line is gathered slowly into your left hand. No matter which retrieve you use, if strikes don't come, try varying the speed of the retrieve. Speeding up will often produce strikes. Yet, at other times, you must use a very slow retrieve to get results. Remember, the fly must look natural, it must swim. If the fly is allowed only to sit, it will never produce a strike from a fish.

EQUIPMENT

No hard and fast rule governs your choice of gear for lake fishing. There will be times, especially in small ponds, when delicate fly rods will be more successful, but for the most part I like to fish lakes with a rod slightly more powerful and longer than one I would use for a normal stream. A rod eight-and-a-half to nine feet, handling at least a seven-weight line is usually a good choice. The more powerful rods are better for making longer casts and for fighting the larger fish often found in impoundment.

Even more important in lake fishing is your choice of fly line. I prefer a weight-forward fly line to a double-taper—once again for its ability to cast greater distances. It is imperative that you reach the fish. Nothing is more frustrating that to find yourself casting ten feet short of where you know the fish are. Besides a floating fly line, I like to carry both slow- and fast-sink lines for fishing the various depths of the lake. High-density, or extremely fast-sinking, fly lines usually are not necessary and can be detrimental. Remember, it is important not only to control the rate of sink, but also to be able to fish the fly at the depth where the fish are located. Therefore, over the years I have found a slow-sinking line the best. It allows the fly to remain at a particular level for a long time without sinking beyond it.

A general, single action trout reel is more than adequate. Make sure it has enough line capacity to handle a very large trout. At least 100 yards of backing may be required, and small reels simply won't do the job. I've had fish run 150 to 200 yards in a lake. Without sufficient reel capacity and adequate backing, I would have lost them.

FLOAT TUBES

People fish lakes in different ways. Those who backpack into high mountain lakes are pretty much restricted to wading from shore. Those who can drive to their destinations may use floating devices, either boats or the now very popular float tubes.

In the past 15 years float tubes, or belly boats, have captured the fancy of the fishing fraternity. Today, they are manufactured far and wide, with innovations designed to provide comfort and convenience while fishing. They come with back rests, which also act as backup floatation for emergencies, big pockets for carrying fly boxes, aprons to collect fly line as it is stripped from the reel, and rodholders.

Quite safe, float tubes were involved in only one death that I know of, and in that case it was cardiac arrest that ended the fisherman's life before the tube tipped over. Indeed, it is probably accurate to say that float tubes are at times safer than boats, especially when an unexpected storm materializes. Float tubes will ride the swells, while a boat can easily be swamped. As an added protection (and some states now require it), you can wear a flotation vest.

Float tubes.
Float tubes, or "belly boats," provide anglers access to places in lakes and slow-moving deep streams unavailable to them by wading. Too, they afford anglers a lower profile in the water than do boats or wading.

12

Warmwater Fishing

Warmwater fishing, or more specifically the pursuit of bass and panfish, has more active participants in the United States than any other type of fishing. Fly fishing often calls to mind pictures of trout streams, but unfortunately these waters are found only in isolated pockets, mostly in the northern part of the country. A good portion of the American fishing population has little access to the scenic and idyllic pastime of trout fishing. Furthermore, because many of the great trout streams are under some sort of duress from pollution and/or alteration, that fishery is shrinking; we can expect the importance of warmwater fishing to increase as more and more mountain-fed streams succumb to human shortsightedness.

Even with the most modern technology, man is simply unable to replicate a stream environment, the product of millions of years of work by Mother Nature. That is not the case when it comes to warmwater fisheries. Dams and irrigation projects, which create massive reservoirs and impoundments, add tremendously to warmwater fisheries in the United States. Moreover, much of the United States has temperatures ideal for nurturing warmwater species. Consequently, bass and panfish today are thriving in great numbers.

It has always been puzzling to me why the fly rod has only lately been used by warmwater anglers. I started fly fishing for bass as a diversion from my life as a trout fisherman. Soon, I recognized both the fun and the challenge that warmwater fish present. Casting to largemouth bass with surface plugs or to smallmouth bass with small nymphs and streamers—even finding massive schools of bluegill—can be as much fun as any kind of angling I know.

Warmwater fisheries are made up of species that adapt to waters in the 65 to 75 degree range. In that category are both large and smallmouth bass and

Fishing in lily pads for bass and other warmwater species often requires pinpoint casting technique.

a host of panfish, primarily bluegill and crappie. Each of these species has its own habits, environment, and angling technique, so each needs to be considered individually before you cast to it with a fly.

LARGEMOUTH BASS

There are many species and subspecies of bass—striped, florida and white, to name a few—but it is the largemouth that most think of as the bass. We tend to think of bass as originating in the southern United States, but surprisingly many of the species come from the north, specifically northern Ontario, the Great Lakes, and the tributaries of the Ohio River. Largemouths prefer, and are generally found, in fairly shallow, weedy lakes that rarely exceed 30 to 35 feet in depth. They will often locate themselves in the weediest parts of the impoundment, as this is where most of their food sources are found. Migration to deeper parts of the lake also occurs according to temperature variations during certain parts of the season. Like all lake fish, largemouth seek the optimum thermoclines where oxygen, temperature, and light penetration make for the most comfort. But as a general rule, you can bet that bass will not venture too far away from vegetation and food.

The largemouth is widely distributed throughout the United States. Today it is found in almost every state in the Union, but the South is where the very large bass, some exceeding 20 pounds, are taken. In the north, a largemouth of more than four pounds is somewhat rare.

Largemouth bass.

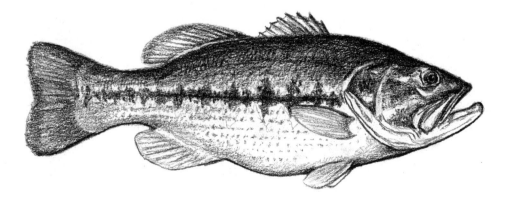

A spring spawner, the largemouth goes to its spawning beds as early as February in the South and as late as mid-June up north. The most productive time to fish for bass is in the spring, or during pre- and post-spawning when the bass move into the shallows to create their beds. Discovering their spawning beds is the important first step for fishing spring bass with a fly.

Locations

Understanding where to find the largemouth is not much different from discerning the location of any other fish within a lake. A review of the chapter on fishing for lake fish will give you an insight as to the holding waters of largemouth bass. Other than weedy areas, likely holding spots include points of land, shallows, creek inlets, drop-offs, and any place where grasses and lily pads are visible. Electronic fish locaters have greatly eased the problem of reading structure and are also a help in locating the fish themselves.

Knowledge of food sources is also important. In the bass's infant stage, its diet consists primarily of insects and crustaceans. As the fish grows in size its diet changes to crayfish, frogs, and other fish. Because of this wide array of food, many kinds of fly imitations present opportunities to a bass flyrodder.

EQUIPMENT FOR FISHING
THE LARGEMOUTH BASS

Because of the fish's size—and often its location—your bass fly rodding equipment needs to be stouter than what is normally used for general trout fishing. I prefer a fly rod of eight-and-a-half to nine-and-a-half feet in length that will handle either a seven- or an eight-weight line. The rod must be fairly stiff for casting the bulky flies commonly used for bass and for moving the fish away from the entanglements of its usual habitat.

For working in shallows, the floating fly line is your most important weapon, but you should also carry sinking lines in case the fish have migrated to cooler and deeper water. The line should have a bass-bug taper, that is to say, a shorter and bulkier weight-forward fly line that will enable you to easily cast and turn over the bulky, wind-resistant flies.

In general, leaders should be fairly short, about seven-and-a-half feet, tapered to a fairly stout tippet in the six- to 15-pound test range. I was once fishing for bass in a newly formed and now-famous reservoir in Texas containing an immense amount of flooded timber. After losing ten-odd bass to the underwater forestry, I finally conceded that a strong leader was necessary. I settled on a tippet point in the 15-pound range, which enabled me to pull the fish from among the menacing snags.

Flies

As mentioned, largemouth bass eat just about anything they can get into their mouths. Thus, the array of imitations possible is just about endless. Both surface and subsurface flies can be used, for there are times when each will be appropriate, but it is the surface popping bugs that offer one of the greatest thrills in fishing. When a largemouth bass explodes the surface attacking a twitched popper among the lily pads, it can leave your heart in your throat.

Surface or floating-type flies consist mainly of popping bugs, meant to imitate frogs, field mice, or other creatures that enter the water from above. They come in a variety of sizes and shapes. It is the slight, often angled indentation at the front of the popper that creates the "pop" or "slurp" as the fly is retrieved along the surface.

Popper technique varies with the angler, but I have found my greatest success comes when, after delivering the fly to a selected spot, I quickly snap the rod tip up, giving the fly the initial pop that gets the bass' attention. After the pop I twitch the rod back and forth, making the popper quiver in the water. This twitching usually induces the powerful strike from the fish. The most

Largemouth Flies and Poppers

A typical selection of largemouth flies includes bugs, minnows, shrimp, streamers, and poppers.

important thing is for the fly to look alive, and this twitching motion brings on this result.

Subsurface flies consist of patterns that imitate leeches, crayfish, eelworms, and other fish. Many of the flies we use for trout can therefore be adapted for bass fishing. Various streamers, such as the muddler, the marabou muddler minnows, light and dark spruce flies, large leech patterns, woolly buggers, and woolly worms are often extremely effective. The flies should be fished in hook sizes in the four to six range, and should come equipped with weed guards, protecting the hook from snagging on underwater plants.

When fishing subsurface flies, the speed of the retrieve is probably as important as the fly itself. You'll often need to experiment to discover which retrieve will induce the most strikes. I have found that bass prefer a slow-moving fly; but there will be times when the fly must be ripped through the water as quickly as you can strip your line. Also, an even retrieve with various hesitations will induce bass to strike.

Whatever method, surface or subsurface, you choose, the largemouth is certainly a worthy prey and the true monarch of our warmwater species. Those who have never pursued it with a flyrod are missing one of the great experiences in angling.

SMALLMOUTH BASS

The smallmouth bass differs in appearance from the largemouth in that its upper jaw does not extend beyond the eye. Like the largemouth, the small-mouth bass has adapted well to warmer water streams throughout the country. The smallmouth also originated in the upper Great Lake/Ohio River drainages, and its early and wide distribution is attributed to the expansion of our railroad system. Undoubtedly, it was the gandy dancers, working along the railroads, who, wishing to extend their fishing opportunities into newly opened lands, carried the smallmouth into habitats where they subsequently flourished.

Smallmouth bass.

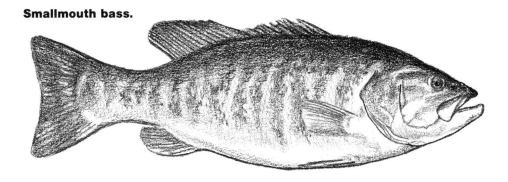

In a lake situation, smallmouth differ from largemouth in their choice of location. They prefer lakes deeper than 30 feet and frequent much rockier, less vegetated areas. In rivers (common to smallmouths), they look for the quiet spots where the current has been slowed by backeddies, large boulders, and the like. Don't look for them where the current moves quickly. Reading water will be extremely important if you are to locate these prize fish in a stream.

EQUIPMENT FOR FISHING SMALLMOUTH BASS

Because smallmouth bass do not reach the tremendous sizes that largemouth do, you can use more or less the same equipment as you would for trout fishing, preferably an eight to eight-and-a-half foot rod throwing a six- or seven-weight line. Floating and sink-tip fly lines should be adequate for river situations, but if you fish for smallmouth in a lake, you will often find them at depths reachable only by fast, even, high-density sinking lines.

In a river, your leader should be adaptable to the surrounding situation. Where the water is very clear, light leaders may be necessary, just as with most trout fishing. The ideal tippet points for smallmouth fishing range from 3x to 5x in diameter. On a lake I will often use a heavier leader to accommodate large, bulky flies at depth.

Flies for Fishing Smallmouth Bass

In a river environment, smallmouth often take the same flies used for trout fishing. Hairwing-type dry flies, such as the Wulff patterns or Humpy's, can be used when surface activity is prevalent. Various nymphs, ranging in size from eights through 12s, are also effective. Because smallmouth will feed on different types of minnows in both rivers and lakes, small streamers such as muddlers and bucktails work quite well. Woolly worms and woolly buggers in smaller sizes should also be on your list of subsurface fare.

Fishing for smallmouth bass with a fly rod is great fun. They readily accept flies and can be just as cagy as the most selective trout. Once you make the commitment to locating these fish, the experience will most certainly be gratifying.

BLUEGILL AND CRAPPIE

A fisherman whom I respect once made a revealing statement to me: "If you want to teach someone to catch fish on a fly rod, put him in a boat and let him drop a fly in a covey of bluegill in the springtime." He was so right! Because panfish multiply to such great numbers, once you have located their position, you are likely to get a strike on just about every cast. In the panfish category, crappie and bluegill reign supreme.

The crappie is one of the largest of panfish, often exceeding two-and-a-half pounds. Like many warmwater fish, it originated in the northern United States but was quickly adapted to the tepid waters of lakes and farm ponds in almost every state.

The bluegill is by far the most widely distributed fish in the country. It is easily distinguished from the crappie by its blue tint and dark blue flap on the gill plate, as well as its smaller size. Both fish have a tendency to overpopulate a lake, and when they are introduced to an impoundment, only a lack of water can drive them out. Therefore, a few fish taken home for dinner will not hurt the population and may very likely help relieve an overpopulation problem. As

Bluegill.

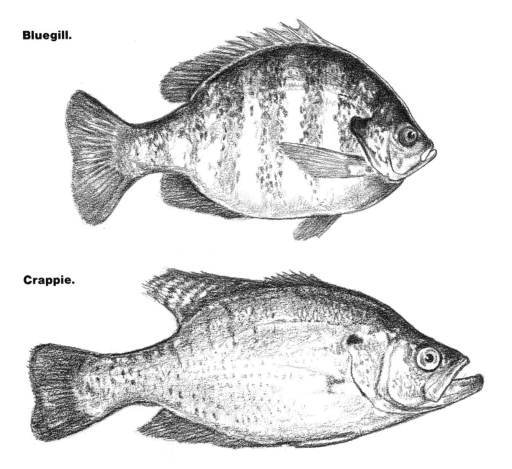

Crappie.

fish go, bluegill or crappie fillets deep fried make as fine a meal as one can find.

Both bluegill and crappie are schooling fish: Where you find one you will find many more. In the spring, when both do their spawning, they can be found in the very shallow, rocky, shoreline waters of lakes and ponds, as well as in small inlet streams. During the warmer weeks of summer, bluegill and crappie will locate in the deeper parts of the lake, preferring to hide in various types of underwater structures. Panfish anglers will often create habitat for both species by dropping brushpiles into lakes. Find these spots and you are likely to be in for a panfish delight.

EQUIPMENT FOR FISHING BLUEGILL AND CRAPPIE

These small fish can be taken on light trout fishing gear. The lighter the rod, the greater the fight—and the better the fun. I prefer a rod of seven-and-a-half to eight feet that throws a four- to five-weight line. A floating line is usually all that is necessary, but occasionally a sink-tip or full-sinking line is needed to reach either species in deeper water.

Bluegill and crappie are not terribly leader-shy, so that leaders tippets in the 2x to 3x category can be used. Also, because these fish are often found in shallow, grassy parts of lakes and ponds, a stout leader may well be needed to pull the fly and the fish out of the weeds.

Flies

Since insects make up the primary diet of both bluegill and crappie, many of our trout flies, both dry and wet, will work well. Dry flies should consist of small, bushy patterns that imitate both mayfly and caddis. Small popping bugs, retrieved and twitched in the same manner you use for bass, also produce delightful dry fly or surface action.

Subsurface patterns should be small nymphs and leech patterns tied in various colorations, from yellow to dark brown. They should be retrieved as you would for any other lake or pond fishing, although when you have located the fish in deep water, a weighted fly retrieved with a jigging motion is often more successful than a regular retrieve. To jig the fly, I add a piece of splitshot just above the fly and drop it straight down into the area where the fish are schooling. By snapping the rod tip up and gently letting the fly bounce down, you will produce strikes.

Because crappie reach larger sizes, they sometimes feed on small minnow.

Whether the fish you catch is big or small, warm-water fishing is always what any angling should be: fun.

If crappie is your main pursuit, a few small streamer and bucktail type flies should be in your arsenal to attract the attention of larger fish. Retrieve these in the manner that makes them appear most natural.

Whether it is bluegill or crappie that you choose to pursue, these fish will add much to your fly rod fun. I look forward to fishing for them every spring, both for the eating and for the exhilaration of throwing my line into a school of these dynamite fish.

Warmwater species in general are bound to become more popular among fly fishermen as the years go on. I know from experience that if you try it once, you will be addicted.

13

Salmon, Steelhead, and Saltwater Fly Fishing

All fish have migratory tendencies. For some, the migration is limited to the stream: moving from one holding lie to another and later to spawning beds. For others the movement is from the stream to larger bodies of water, such as lakes and man-made impoundments. But for a small group of fish, migration is epic: from the small streams and rivers where they are reared to the unlimited reaches of the oceans, where they spend the greatest portion of their lives. Many fish belong to this latter category, but when we think of sea-run fish, it is the Atlantic and Pacific salmon and the steelhead that come immediately to mind.

Owing to their immense power, strength and beauty, these fish are pursued by a small, avid corps of fishermen on both the east and west coasts of the United States, as well as in parts of Europe. Traditions for both Atlantic salmon and steelhead are rich, having been made bigger than life by such authors as Zane Grey and Roderick Haig-Brown. As long as our coastal river systems remain intact and are properly managed, these traditions should continue and grow.

ATLANTIC SALMON
(Salmo salar)

The Atlantic salmon must be considered the aristocrat of all migratory fish, for it has been searched out by fishermen from all walks of life for hundreds of years. Of the family *salmonidae,* the Atlantic salmon is found throughout many northern American river systems from Cape Cod through Canada and as far north as Greenland. In Europe, its range extends from as far south as Portugal to Norway in the north, although the central European countries, which by and

A sea-run fish, the majestic Atlantic salmon can be found at particular times during the year in coastal rivers such as this one in eastern Canada.

Atlantic salmon.

large have permitted the degradation of their streams, have watched the demise of their once-abundant salmon runs.

Like most other migratory fish, the Atlantic salmon has long been pursued both for sport and for its commercial value. For years, fishermen on both sides of the Atlantic were puzzled as to the salmon's winter grounds. Finally, in the 1970s, the salmon were discovered in great numbers off the coast of Greenland, creating a frenzy of commercial activity that resulted in a severe reduction in the species' population. Only in the last several years, through efforts of the Atlantic Salmon Foundation, has this great fish begun to enjoy some protection from human greed.

The Atlantic salmon spawns in the tributaries of North American and European rivers. Leaving the freshwater system as a smolt, it reaches sexual maturity after three to five years and then returns to the river system of its birth to spawn. Those that return after only one year at sea are generally smaller, four pounds average, and are called "grilse." Those that spend at least two winters in the ocean return as nine- to 12-pound fish. Yet a third group, after three or four years at sea, return as 20- to 40-pound salmon. Individuals in this third class can grow as large as 70 pounds, with Norway renowned as the place to find these giants.

SALMON LOCATION AND FISHING APPROACH

Upon reentering the river system, the Atlantic salmon will seek out traditional holding and resting lies on their way upstream to spawn. They usually hold in the quieter portions of a stream, often in shallow water or a slight depression in the river bottom. The migratory route can be quite long, so a good guide or friend who knows the waters can be helpful in pointing out where to fish or not to fish.

Salmon do not feed while in the river system, and among fishermen it has always been a matter of some discussion as to why they will take the fly. Some believe it is a throwback to behavior learned as river smolt. Others think that it is with their mouths that the fish satisfy their curiosity about objects in the water. No one really knows, but it is a happy anomaly that Atlantic salmon will accept an artificial.

One of the most important elements in fishing for Atlantic salmon is persistence. Those who are accustomed to fishing for trout typically lay a fly over a fish or a suspected lie two or three times before moving on to another target. But with the Atlantic salmon the fly may be presented 20, 30, or even 40 times before it takes an interest. It is thus important to *keep working the fish or the line for a reasonable length of time.*

Technique varies among river systems, but two methods of fishing the fly are generally followed: (1) the greaseline, or Woods (see wet fly fishing, page 135) method, and (2) the Crosfield, or swinging fly technique. Regardless of which method you use, most experts believe that *the speed of the fly in the water is crucial to producing a strike.* Also, presenting the fly broadside to the fish, or where the fish can view the complete outline of the fly, is very important.

In both methods, the fly is presented across and slightly downstream. In greaselining, the line is continually mended, allowing the fly to drift slowly, rather than swing, into the holding spot. This technique naturally creates a broadside fly approach. In the Crosfield technique, the fly is allowed to swing with the current over the suspected holding water without any mending. Regardless of which method is employed, it is always important that at the end of the drift the fly be allowed to hang in the current, for many fish will take at this crucial position.

Large dry flies can be used to take salmon. The technique is largely the same as described above: Cast across and slightly downstream and allow the fly to drift over the hold. Whether you fish dry or wet flies, don't forget that you must persist longer over salmon than you would for most other fish.

EQUIPMENT FOR SALMON FISHING

Equipment needs vary with the size of fish you are casting to. For small grilse, a nine-and-a-half foot rod that can throw as small as a seven-weight line can be adequate for some fishermen. But, in general, a nine-and-a-half foot rod, throwing a nine- or ten-weight line, is the most common size. The rod must be powerful enough to handle long casts in addition to the powerful strike. On many streams in Norway and Scotland, the two-handed salmon rod of 13 to 16 feet is still a very popular tool.

Most lines used for Atlantic salmon are the floating type, although there are applications for sink-tip lines where water runs deeper. Although double tapers can be used in smaller streams, weight-forward lines are more commonly used.

The fly reel for Atlantic salmon must be of sturdy construction and large enough to hold both fly line and at least 200 yards of 30-pound dacron backing.

Fly leaders should be nine to 12 feet in length and tapered to a tippet point between six- and 12-pound breaking strength, which may vary in x-size from one to another manufacturer. Dry-fly fishing requires leaders of slightly smaller diameter.

Flies

The tradition of Atlantic salmon flies is rich and colorful. For some anglers the very sight of Atlantic salmon patterns is reason enough to pursue these great fish. Traditionally, the old patterns were tied matching exotic feathers to the elegant up-eyed hook. The Jock Scott, Silver Wilkinson, Silver and Gray, Blue Charm, Lady Amherst, and Red Abby are some of the classics in the sport. Today, Hairwing patterns, with hair replacing the traditional feathers, are widely used. Tube flies, with hair and feathers fashioned around a plastic tube through which the leader is passed and attached to the hook, have become extremely popular in Iceland and Norway, as well as in the Canadian provinces.

Today, an assortment of flies for the salmon angler might consist of: Black, Silver, and Rusty Rats; and Green Butt, Black Bear, Cosseboom, Blue Charm, Hairy Mary, Jock Scott, Dusty Miller, and various color combinations of tube flies, ranging in size from 3/0 to 10. A fully prepared salmon fisherman will have them all. He'll also know the river system on which he fishes. North American waters are comparatively smaller than other places where Atlantic salmon run. Flies tied on fours to as small as tens are often used. In Iceland, England, or Norway, the popular sizes are anywhere from 1-0 to 5-0.

In addition to the standard wet fly (very popular among salmon anglers), are low-water patterns. These are small flies tied on oversized hooks. A small assortment in various sizes, tied to the pattern of your choice, should also be carried.

For dry-fly fishing, flies of the Wulff series, such as the Royal, Blond,

Grizzly, and Gray, are very popular. In addition, Irresistibles and Humpies, tied on the traditional light-wire, and up-eyed salmon hooks will be best for those who enjoy surface fishing.

Fishing for Atlantic salmon is the classic of all our angling experiences. It can be costly and, worse, uncertain. But for the most part, the Atlantic salmon is a dream worth sacrificing for. It is often said that catching these fish is a disease—expensive and chronic—but it is something you find difficult to live without.

STEELHEAD

If the Atlantic salmon is king of the Atlantic, the steelhead must be queen of the rivers that feed the Pacific Ocean. My first experience with a steelhead came as a small boy fishing the coastal Northwest waters in Washington state for trout. When I cast a small wet fly onto a large pool, the fly came to a snagging stop. As I tried to wrench it loose, a large silvery fish bolted from the depths with my fly in its mouth and began relieving me of line at an incredible rate. Thinking this must be the largest trout in the world, I fought valiantly until the fish, upon reaching the last turn of line, broke me off with a shrug and disappeared. So powerful was the experience that it has remained vivid in my mind ever since.

The steelhead is actually a sea-run rainbow. Once recognized with its own classification, today it is identified by the scientific name *Salmo gairdneri*— same as the rainbow trout. Its range extends from as far south as northern California, north to Oregon, Idaho, Washington, British Columbia, and into Alaska. Now, through the introduction of steelhead into the Great Lakes, Michigan streams can be added to this list.

Steelhead.

Because the steelhead are often more abundant and their rivers more accessible, they are fished for by many more anglers than the Atlantic salmon. Rivers such as the Rogue, the MacKenzie, the Deschutes, and the North Umpqua, which flows by the legendary Steamboat Inn in Oregon; the Stillaguamish, Solduc, Skagit, and others in the state of Washington; the Dean and, home of perhaps the largest of the steelhead strain, the Kispiox drainage in British Columbia—all are traditional homes of the great sea-run fish.

Upon entering the ocean as smolt, steelhead feed on small fish, squid, and crustaceans, growing to various sizes. The first to return to the rivers are small specimens of no more than four to seven pounds. Referred to as "summer-run" or "A-run" fish, they have spent less than one year in the ocean. The largest steelhead ("winter fish" or "B-run") return after three years at sea. With their acute and highly refined olfactory senses, steelhead generally return to the drainage in which they were reared to deposit their eggs.

There are many different strains, each unique to its own drainage. In Idaho, all the steelhead reach their spawning grounds through the Columbia River system, yet the Clearwater River tributary produces fish of 20 pounds, while the nearby Salmon River breeds smaller ten- to 15-pounders. The same thing happens in river systems throughout Oregon, Washington, and British Columbia, with the Kispiox River continually producing world record specimens.

STEELHEAD LOCATION

Angling techniques and fish location differ depending upon which river system you fish in. Traditionally, steelhead will hold in sections of the river quite different from those where you will find trout. Steelhead seek water where they can rest. After migrating through heavy riffle and whitewater, they are most likely to locate themselves at the tails of pools just above the rapids, or in the side channels. They seek rocks and ledges where the water has slowed. When a steelhead reaches the head of a pool or run, it is generally on its way upstream to its next holding spot and can't be bothered with feeding.

TECHNIQUES FOR STEELHEAD FISHING

One of the most popular methods of fishing for steelhead is the greaseline technique, using floating or intermediate fly line. The fly is presented across and slightly downstream and continually mended upstream so that the fly drifts, rather than drags, through the suspected hold. During the winter months when

Winter is often a productive season for steelheading, and the results can be well worth the cold-water wading.

the fly must be fished deep for maximum success, casting slightly up and across, allowing the fly to sink deep, and mending the line to control the fly's speed is a technique that often works.

With either of the above techniques, the fly should be allowed to hold in the current after it has swung downstream of the angler. Many steelhead will follow the fly, and it is at this point that most strikes occur. Stripping the line a few times and then letting the fly drift back downstream will often induce the fish to take.

Like Atlantic salmon fishing, steelhead fishing requires patience. Steelhead are not so abundant that there will be a fish on every cast. Success is not measured by the number of fish caught or hooked, but rather by the experience itself. Once you have hooked a steelhead, you will know exactly what I mean.

EQUIPMENT FOR STEELHEAD FISHING

Tackle for steelhead is not much different from what you would use to catch Atlantic salmon. Rods can be as small as eight-foot throwing six- or seven-weight lines or as large as nine to 10½ feet, handling nine- and ten-weight line. I recommend the latter sizes in anticipation of hooking and handling a big fish. Anything less than an eight-weight line is usually inadequate.

The steelhead fisherman should have a complete array of fly lines, ranging from floating to high-density sink-tips and full sinking high-density lines. A recent innovation, available through various small companies, is the lead-core sinking fly line, which allows you to reach the very bottom of the very big water.

Without question, weight-forward line taper is more successful than double taper because of the casting distances involved. Being able to competently perform the double haul cast will also greatly enhance your ability to reach and fish the big waters where steelhead will hold. Shooting heads, or lines of 30 feet in length, which are attached to a monofilament running line, are used, but unfortunately they afford scant means of controlling the drift of the fly. They are most successful in river systems that are big, deep, and characterized by relatively even current flow. Split shot, a.k.a. split head, should be carried for even greater depth.

As with Atlantic salmon, your reels should be sturdy with plenty of capacity to handle the long runs these steelhead often make. There should be room for your fly line and 150 to 200 yards of 30-pound dacron.

Leaders range between five and 12 feet in length, depending on the type of fishing you will be doing. Very short leaders are more successful with full sinking fly lines, allowing the fly to reach the bottom at roughly the same rate as the line. Longer leaders—seven-and-a-half to nine feet—should be used with floating or sink-tip fly lines. Your tippet points: six to 14 pounds test.

Steelhead Flies

As with Atlantic salmon, a great tradition has developed around steelhead flies. Unlike Atlantic salmon, the steelhead will feed to various types of insects while migrating upstream to spawn, although spawning tends to take priority over feeding. Years ago, flies were tied in brightly colored patterns imitating such things as egg roe and shrimp. Against the typical rainy-gray days characteristic of the Northwest, these flies are highly visible. The Skykomish Sunrise, Thor, Babine Special, Kispiox Special, McCloud's Ugly, Purple Peril, Umpqua Special, Silver Hilton, and Green Butted Skunk are but a few of the successful patterns used over the years. Knowing steelhead feed during spawning runs, today's anglers are also taking a more natural approach to flies, offering patterns such as sparsely tied muddlers and soft tackle flies, which imitate the various larvae of caddis and terrestrials. The now popular single egg flies, tied in various colors, are equally important.

Fly size depends on the river system and water conditions. An assortment of the above-mentioned patterns in sizes four through eight are the generally accepted arsenal.

In the past, dry flies were used for the smaller summer-run fish in low-water conditions, but today surface patterns are a popular method of pursuing all steelhead in all types of water conditions. Patterns consist of the traditional Wulff, with the Royal Wulff favored over all others. Various grasshopper flies, and large caddisflies, imitating the rust-colored *Dicosmoecus,* which hatches in late fall coincidental with steelhead runs, are also productive.

Your dry fly technique will need some modification for steelhead. The fish seems to prefer a fly that skitters across the surface as it begins its swing below the angler. Casting across and slightly downstream, you should try to impart some erratic movement with the rodtip as the fly passes over a suspected hold of water. The motion seems to get their attention and often induces a strike.

The steelhead is certainly one of the most popular of the large migratory fish pursued by fly fishermen. It is accessible and fairly abundant. If man can curb his tendency to block the fish's migratory routes with dams, we should have steelhead in our streams forever.

PACIFIC SALMON

Pacific salmon were not always a realistic goal for fly fishermen, but with the modern innovations in fly lines and fly rods, these magnificent fish are now within reach of growing numbers of fly anglers. Pacific salmon come in five species: pink, chum, sockeye, silver or coho, and chinook. The West Coast from northern California to Alaska has always been their haven, but in recent years some species have been successfully introduced to the Great Lakes drainages, bringing exciting fly fishing to a great number of anglers in the Midwest. Today the really great salmon fishing is found in Alaska. When the salmon arrive in the various river systems feeding the Bristol Bay area, they can overwhelm the watercourse. If you stand on a high bank overlooking one of these streams, the river, right to its bottom, will appear to be in perpetual turbulence.

Although different species of salmon are pursued with a fly, the chinook and silver are probably the most popular. Entering the river in early summer, chinooks can generally be found from early July on. They are quickly followed by silvers in August.

Fall and winter spawners, these fish readily accept a fly and when hooked can create tackle-busting experiences. Like the Atlantic Salmon, Pacific Salmon do not feed when they enter the freshwater system. Consequently, their reason for taking a fly is not fully understood. The successful flies tend to be brightly colored, resembling the egg masses that are constantly being emitted by the females on their journey upstream. Egg-sperm flies and various egg patterns, tied on hook sizes from 1-0 to 4, are the types most often used. Small streamers, such as the Comet series, as well as larger Black Leeches and Woolly Buggers, will also take fish.

Chinooks typically hold in deep water and seldom, if ever, move to the surface for a fly, making sinking fly lines necessary to reach them. Variations of lead-core, which reach the bottom quickly, are being used more frequently today. Floating lines will also work if the fish are found in shallow streams.

Equipment for kings has to be powerful. Anything less than a rod of nine-and-a-half feet, powerful enough to handle a 10-weight line, is just not adequate. Sturdy reels, with a capacity of 200 yards of backing, are also standard operating equipment. Leaders should be between four and seven-and-a-half feet in length, allowing the fly to reach the bottom quickly. They should be between 12 and 20 pounds in breaking strength. This heavy equipment is necessary, for the runs of a king salmon can be likened to hooking onto a freight train. As the line disappears from your reel you wonder whether anything will be able to stop these fish. And many times they do prove to be unstoppable.

Silver, or coho, salmon are among the more delightful fish to catch on a fly rod. They accept flies readily, their runs are long and powerful, and they may even outperform the rainbow in acrobatic maneuvering. Most silvers enter the river systems in August for fall and winter spawning. At maturity, they weigh between six and 12 pounds. Equipment needn't be as powerful as that used for a chinook, with rods in the eight-and-a-half to nine-foot category, handling eight- and nine-weight lines, most often used.

Floating and sinking fly lines are used with success, depending on the type of water. I have taken a multitude of silvers using floating lines, but generally some type of sinking line is needed for maximum success. Reels, once again, should be sturdy and should have enough spool capacity to handle long runs.

Choice of coho flies is wide-open to debate. I have taken silvers on a full array of patterns, so it is difficult to recommend any one thing. Egg flies are successful, but because silvers seem more willing to feed than other salmon, bucktail and streamer type flies work surprisingly well, too. In addition, various black leech patterns tied on 1-0 to 4 hooks have, in recent years, been very effective.

Angler Fred Arbona, Jr. and his catch: a 45-pound chinook salmon.

Pacific salmon of all species can provide some of the most exciting fly fishing available to us. In those river systems where they are plentiful, constant hookups can be the rule. The fish are strong and exciting. If you get an opportunity to fish for them, take it. They won't disappoint you.

SALTWATER FLY FISHING

Fly fishing for trout has a very long and rich tradition, but the use of a fly in salt water has a relatively short history. Product development has enabled more and more anglers to pursue saltwater fish, whether they are found inshore or offshore.

In the 1930s there were a few pioneers who ventured into salt water with a fly rod. But because of the inadequate equipment, more successful ocean fishing was done with heavy rods, large level wind reels, and big boats. It was not until the late 1940s and '50s that saltwater fly fishing began to take on new meaning and challenges for anglers. Joe Brooks was among the first to break ground in saltwater fly fishing, and many of his flies and techniques are still used today.

My first experience in salt water was unforgettable. It came relatively late

Saltwater Fly Fishing

Besides angling for deepwater species, many saltwater fly fishermen enjoy "fishing the flats," via either wading (above) or casting from a shallow-draft skiff (below).
The object of their angling: bonefish (above right), permit (below right), and tarpon.

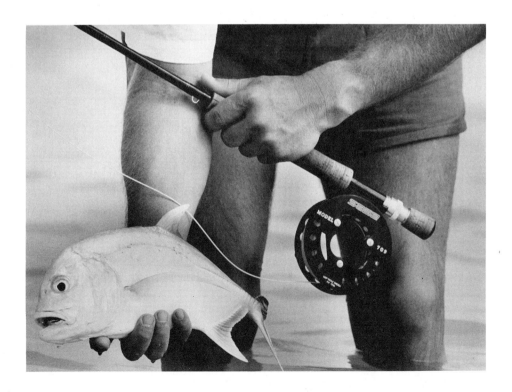

in my life. I was informed that, once I tried it, regardless of the type of fish or its size, fly fishing for anything else might well become meaningless. While fishing for bonita off the coast of Southern California, I was simply amazed that a five-pound fish could take a large fly rod and double it over. Later I pursued tarpon. I didn't land the first ones, but the tarpon we jumped off Key West, Florida, left me awestruck. Seeing a tarpon follow the fly, take it, and then explode from the water's surface gave the sport of fly fishing a new dimension. The experience set my knees to shaking, and the memory remains vivid in my mind.

Innumerable types of fish swimming in the oceans can be pursued with a fly rod. Most are found off both the east and west coasts, in the Gulf of Mexico, and in the Sea of Cortez. Unfortunately, we cannot devote time and space to all the fish that swim our oceans, so I will concentrate on the more important species that are actively fished.

The types of water where saltwater fish are pursued are classified as *offshore, inshore, estuary,* and *shoreline.* Offshore fish include marlin, sailfish, dolphin, wahoo, albacore, bonita, and tuna. Locating offshore fish is done by actually sighting feeding fish, chumming the water, or, in the case of sailfish and marlin, trolling a hookless teaser baitfish through the water and repeatedly taking it away until the fish is lured into casting range. Shipwrecks and reefs are also important grounds for offshore species.

Inshore fishing is synonymous with "fishing the flats." Fish move out of the deeper water into vast flats that may be anywhere from two to 12 feet deep. Tarpon, bonefish, permit, barracuda, and some shark are the species most commonly found.

Fish location is done by sight. Once sighted, the fish are ferreted out and stalked from a small boat or skiff. Because the water is shallow, the angler must be able to deliver the fly very quickly and with little disturbance.

Fishing estuaries—the brackish mix of fresh and salt water—is also very popular and productive. Fish such as snook and baby tarpon move into the canals and estuaries for feeding and often get within easy range of avid anglers.

Shoreline fishing is popular on both coasts. Fish will often move into the surf or along the rocky coves for feeding and are easily reached either from shore or from small skiffs. Bluefish of the Atlantic coast are commonly caught by this method. West Coast striped bass, which hold around inner bay pilings and along rocky shorelines, are a classic example of a shoreline fish species.

Whether you fish offshore, inshore, in estuaries, or along the shoreline, your fly rod equipment must be far sturdier than that used for general trout fishing, since the fish are large and powerful.

Rods, Lines, and Reels

For years very big rods were thought to be a must for saltwater fly fishing. But today you will find a full array of rod sizes appropriate for the various fish. Most rods are nine-and-a-half to ten feet long and cast a nine- to 13-weight line, the latter for tarpon and marlin, the former for smaller bonefish. It's important to note that, especially with the larger rods, it's less your casting, but more your fighting and fish-lifting ability that are important.

Various densities of sinking lines are useful, especially for offshore deep water fish, but in most cases, intermediate, or very slow-sinking, fly lines are preferred. Intermediate lines sink slowly and, if dressed, float. All should be a saltwater taper. Fly line color is also important. Avoid bright colors, such as white, yellow, and the fluorescent greens and oranges that are sometimes used for trout fishing. Blues and grays are more appropriate and successful.

The fly reel may be your most important piece of equipment. It has to be extremely durable, capable of handling the devastating run of many saltwater species. I have seen inexpensive reels soften, bend, and seize up, with relatively small saltwater fish. Most saltwater reels have a disc brake system that allows you to put great pressure on a fish without freezing the reel. Most saltwater reels are expensive, but the investment is justified. Whichever reel you choose, it should have sufficient capacity to hold at least 250 yards of 30-pound dacron backing. Many times I have wanted even more, much more.

Saltwater reels.
Though expensive, these corrosion-resistant reels are essential for fishing in saltwater conditions.

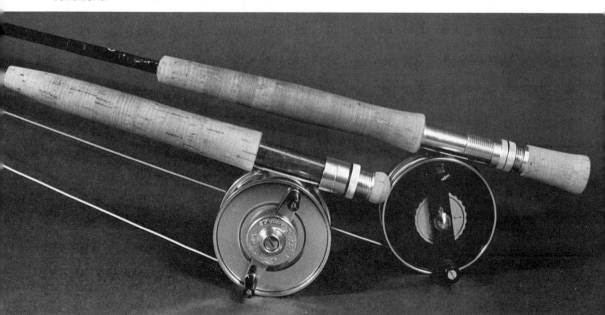

Saltwater Leaders

Due to the size, power, and the tackle-destructive behavior of many saltwater fish, special considerations should be given to the fly leader used to subdue these fish. Because saltwater flies are big, bulky, and often heavy, a sophisticated tapered trout fishing leader is unimportant. What is important to the saltwater angler is a leader that protects against the fish and the knots that hold the entire monofilament sections together.

Most saltwater leaders range between nine and 12 feet in length, with the longer ones being used in water conditions where the fish frighten easily. Although there are leaders of tapered multiple-piece construction (especially when bonefish and permit are pursued), most saltwater leaders are of the three-piece types. In a simplified form, the three-piece leader consists of a running line, which is connected to the fly line; a tippet class section, which is the actual pound test being used; and a special shock tippet, consisting of either heavy monofilament or wire in the 40 to 80-pound class. This shock section protects against sharp teeth, bills, gill-plates, and the skin texture often found in saltwater fish. These three sections are often joined together by using an Albright knot.

A more sophisticated three-piece leader that is used more often and has become synonymous with saltwater fly fishing consists of the Bimini twist knot that is tied at both ends of the tippet class section. Fishermen, either freshwater or saltwater, quickly learn that knots are the weak link in any leader arrangement. When constructed properly, the Bimini does not lessen the actual breaking strength of the class section. Consequently, it's often referred to as the 100 percent knot. To connect the running line and shock tippet to the Biminied class section, either an Albright or an offset nail knot is often used. Because the Bimini twist creates a loop, a quick change loop to loop connection can also be employed. The latter connection is fine for joining the class and running portion, but I do not suggest it for joining the class to shock sections. When world records are not the aim of the angler, the above mentioned sections can be of any desired length. But, if a world record catch on a particular pound test is desired, you must conform to International Game Fish Association standards before it can be recognized.

The IGFA does not dictate how a leader should be constructed in terms of knots and overall length, but it does standardize both the various line sizes (pound test) and the minimum and maximum length of various sections. The tippet class categories consists of 2, 4, 8, 12, and 16 pounds and must be a minimum of 15 inches measured from the inside of the knots. The shock tippet can consist of either mono or wire in any pound test but cannot be any longer

Saltwater Leaders

Simple, three-piece type.

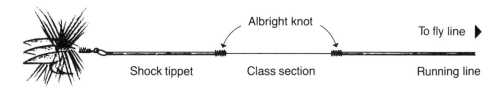

I.G.F.A. type.

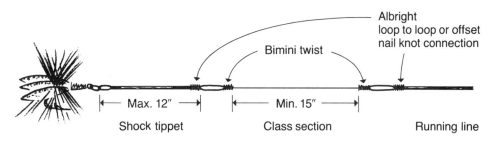

When fishing saltwater for the first time, consider working with a knowledgeable guide who can assist you in locating fish, tying on leaders, choosing flies, and casting properly.

than 12 inches (measured from the eye of the hook up to and including the knot joining the tippet class section).

Unfortunately, because of lack of space, diagramming the construction of the knots mentioned above is impossible. If you do venture out into salt water, though, I urge that you become familiar with the tying procedures. Many books on the market describe, in detail, how these knots are tied.

Saltwater Flies

Because of the diversity of food in salt water, fly patterns for saltwater fishing should be kept relatively simple in conception and construction. More complex, thought-out patterns are used in specific situations, but tying these remains a fairly arcane art. Saltwater flies are tied on special stainless steel or cadmium-plated hooks that can consistently withstand saltwater corrosion. Hook sizes range from as small as 4s and 6s for bonefish, to as large as 3/0 and 8/0, for tarpon and marlin. Most flies imitate various baitfish, eels, shrimp, and crabs. Color combinations such as blue-and-white, red-and-white, and red-and-yellow are used to attract the attention of fish. In some cases, big popping bugs can be used for surface activity. Because saltwater fish generally have bony, hard mouths, saltwater hooks must be razor sharp and must be constantly maintained. For best results, use a hook with a sharp cutting edge configuration.

FISH, FLIES, AND TECHNIQUE FOR SALTWATER FISHING

Because different fish types require unique techniques and equipment setups, the following is a brief overview of the important saltwater fishes, their angling techniques, the necessary equipment, and the flies that are used to take them.

• *Bonefish*—A very exciting fish to catch. As in trout fishing, bonefish angling becomes a hunting, stalking, and casting situation. Pursued on shallow flats where it can be seen rooting through sand for crabs, shrimp, and small baitfish. Tackle should be fairly light, for the fish will range in size from five to 12 pounds. Presentation critical. Cast must lead traveling fish, and presentation must not overly disturb water. Flies can range from 1/0 to 6, depending on the size fish pursued. Most popular places: Florida, Mexico, Belize, Christmas Islands.

Bonefish.

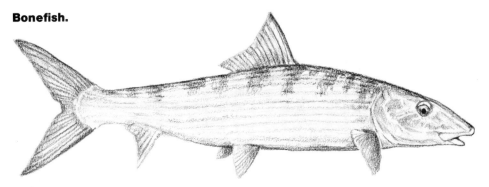

• *Bluefish*—Not readily found, but when located, can be fine game for flyrodder. Commonly found on Atlantic coast from Connecticut through the Carolinas. Generally, a shore-break fish that moves in to work baitfish along shoreline. Has very sharp teeth, so between 40- and 80-pound wire shock tippet is needed. Flies should consist of feathered streamer patterns in all-white and in combinations of yellow-and-white and red-and-white. Technique: Find schooling fish and cast to the middle of them; retrieve very quick and fast.

Bluefish.

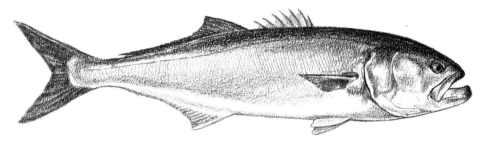

• *Barracuda*—Commonly found on flats. Exciting fish on fly rod and will accept flies readily. Medium tackle with rods that throw between a ten- and 12-weight line needed. Fly patterns are best used on hooks from 1-0 to 3-0, consisting of feathered streamers and, more precisely, eel-type patterns tied as long as 12 inches. Popping bugs can be used. Cannot strip the fly fast enough. Very, very sharp teeth, so 80-pound shock tippet wire is recommended.

• *Tarpon*—Generally regarded as the king of the flats, although they can be found in estuary systems in Florida and in Mexican and Costa Rican waters. Maybe the most spectacular on a fly rod of any of the large fish. Noted for aerial acrobatics. Generally fished when sighted while fish or small school is traveling. Depending on the size of fish, hook size should be 1-0 to 5-0. Various feathered streamers, in combinations of red-and-yellow, all white, blue, red-and-white, blue-and-white, and sometimes green-and-white, will work. Bucktail streamers can also be used. Because of the sharp scales, I recommend using 50- to 80-pound mono shock tippet. Have bony, hard mouths, so hooks must be extremely sharp. Maximum equipment necessary, with rods that throw 12- to 13-weight lines.

Tarpon.

Permit.

• *Permit*—Very difficult to catch on a fly rod. Serious permit anglers count actual fly catches on one hand. Very spooky and seemingly fickle about any single fly pattern. Habitat similar to that of bonefish and can be found in flats as well as in deep water. Shrimp and crab patterns successful, as well as small feathered and Maribou streamers. Hook size from 4 to 1/0. Often heavier flies and/or sinking-type lines necessary to reach these fish, depending on location. Medium tackle recommended. Presents the biggest challenge in salt-water fly fishing.

• *Snook*—Very popular fly rod fish. Found near shallow, sandy beaches, estuaries, and canals throughout Florida. Most range in the ten-pound class, but can be found up to 35 pounds. Readily accept brightly colored flies in sizes 1-0 to 3-0, red and yellow streamers, and popping bugs that are red-and-yellow, red-and-white, and blue-and-white. Because of razor sharp-gill plate, nylon shock tippet of 40 to 60 pounds should be adjacent to the fly. Can be fished both blind and sighted.

• *Striped Bass*—Generally found on West Coast from Oregon south to the San Francisco Bay area and on the East Coast from Maine to Carolinas. Inhabit rocky parts of shoreline, bays, and water around pilings. Have been transplanted to some river systems in the West with great success. Because the fish are usually deep, high-D sinking lines or, more appropriately, lead-core line is often needed. Around rocky shoreline popping bugs have worked, but streamer-type flies, imitating baitfish, are most often used. Fly size or length critical. Flies should be feathered, made of white-and-blue or white-and-green combinations. Fish are large, so 3-0 to 5-0 hooks are the rule.

Striped Bass.

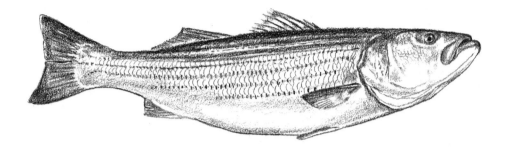

• *Marlin and Sailfish*—Time-consuming work to catch them on fly rod. Most are hooked using the teasing method. Baitfish or feathered jig is trolled without hook and is continually taken away until the fish is within casting range of the boat. Flies consist of very large streamers in combinations of white with blue or green topping. Very large popping bugs are also successful. Hook size 4-0 to 8-0. Because of bill, shock tippet of 80- to 100-pound test nylon recommended.

• *Wahoo*—Difficult fish to hook with fly rod but very exciting. Fish travel in schools. Best success is when one fish is hooked by conventional methods; the other fish will follow hooked fish. Cast the fly in and around area of hooked fish. Flies are large white streamers with either blue or green toppings. Hook size is usually 1-0 to 3-0. Fish have very sharp teeth, so 80- to 100-pound wire shock tippet is required. Cannot retrieve or strip fly quick enough.

• *Shark*—All types can be taken on fly rod. Large and powerful, but cannot see well. Fly must be presented very close to fish, often to one side or the other. Flies consist of brightly colored patterns. Tarpon patterns fairly effective. Wire tippet necessary because of fish's rough skin. Hook sizes range from 5-0 to 7-0. Very exciting fish on a fly.

• *Dolphin (Dorado)*—A fish that loves to school, so once one is hooked many will appear. Prefers brightly colored—red-and-yellow, red-and-orange, red-and-white combinations—flies with 1-0 to 3-0 hook sizes. Does not need a shock tippet; conventional leaders will do the job. Fish will hang under seaweed beds, and selected casts should be made into this area. Fish size into the 40-pound class range.

14

Stream Etiquette and Conservation

The sport of fly fishing is often thought of as a gentlemanly endeavor, pursued with respect for both the surrounding environment and the fish themselves. In addition, the fly fisherman takes great care in all other aspects of the sport, including the equipment he uses and its maintenance, his understanding of the food sources of fish, his use of proper techniques and their refinements. Because the fly fisherman's involvement in his sport is so complete, it is probably fair to say that casting a fly as a means of catching fish is probably performed with greater attention to detail than any other method. And this consciousness naturally extends to matters of stream etiquette, which, in essence, is based pretty much on the good old Golden Rule: To wit, if we observe certain standards of respect and even deference toward our fellow fishermen, then perhaps we will have a right to expect the same from them.

Although not carved in granite, there are a few rules to which we must adhere while sharing the stream (and lake, and saltwater) environment with other people.

Countless stories are told about the rudeness of our fellow fishermen. For the most part, this coarse behavior is not intentional; rather it comes from not understanding the etiquette the sport requires. For some fly fishermen, educating these impertinent souls just isn't their style; but I believe, if we refrain from doing so, the problem of not respecting other people's fishing will remain.

As a general rule all fishermen should be given enough room to carry out their angling as the conditions and location require. Every person has his individual preferences. In the West there are some who like total seclusion and will leave the stream if they see another fisherman. Still others like companionship and camaraderie, also a part of the sport. Not knowing which type you are confronting, you're well advised to avoid crowding and give the other fisherman adequate space to enjoy his sport.

225

Wading into an area being fished by another angler is just plain bad manners.

I once had an experience in which a companion and I had selected a spot containing a few very large fish that we knew would be working during a particular evening hatch. Upon our arrival we found ourselves alone, but after a few minutes another angler appeared, obviously upset that we had taken his spot. Slowly, as the hatch progressed, he made his way, inch by inch, step by step, closer to the rising fish that we were working. Finally, in disgust, I stopped and asked him if he would like to take my location, since he was standing virtually on top of me anyway. To make matters worse, he happened to be an acquaintance and an angler who should have known better. The hard truth is, no matter how many times you have fished a stream or a certain pool, you do not own the river, the location, or the fish. *Whoever is there first gets to fish it.* Respect that right.

Anglers always try to reach the best pool first, before it has been fished by others. But, unfortunately, there will be times when another fisherman occupies your spot when you arrive. The proper thing to do is to wait until your predecessor has completed his stay before even thinking of stepping into the water. Even when the other person appears to have finished up, it is a good idea to ask whether he has completed his fishing before wetting your line. Since he was there first, you must respect his right to fish the pool at his own speed and leisure, regardless of your schedule.

Fly fishing has its contemplative moments, which usually involve sitting on the bank, waiting, and watching, rather than actually fishing. When you encounter such a scene, *you must always ask the other angler his intentions before setting foot in the water.* There is nothing more annoying than when, after you've decided to rest a fish or a run, someone else comes along and starts fishing it. If you respect the other person's reasons for waiting, you will gain a friend.

There is always a question as to who has the right of way when one fisherman is fishing upstream and another is fishing down. Although upstream fishing is prevalent, wet fly and streamer fishing traditionally requires a downstream method. But because greater water disturbance is generated by the downstream angler, and because the upstream working fisherman has greater wading problems, *the upstream working angler has the right of way over someone who is fishing down.* The downstream fisherman should retire from the river or walk around the other angler, avoiding the undue disturbance that his technique often brings.

Wading through a run where another fisherman intends to fish or is already fishing is another common mistake. While fishing the famous Green Drake hatch on the Henry's Fork in Idaho with a fellow guide and store owner,

Mike Lawson of Henry's Fork Anglers, I experienced a classic example of this problem. Upon arriving at the water, we saw other fishermen scattered about, fishing to the selective rises. Now, the Henry's Fork is a wide, but wadable river, and can nicely accommodate a great number of fishermen. We entered the water, and found our own fish to work, but, typical of the Henry's Fork, we also found ourselves near other fishermen. Suddenly, on the bank, a car came roaring to a halt. A person jumped out, scanned the water, quickly donned waders and vest, entered the water, and proceeded to walk right through, not only my fish, but everyone else's as well, putting them all down. Frustrated and a bit amazed, I asked the fisherman what in the hell he was doing. As he kept plowing through the water he turned and said, "Well, I need to get to the other side." If he really needed to do that he should have gone upstream or downstream to cross, avoiding other fishermen. *Do not wade through an area where fishing is taking place.*

Unfortunately, the paths near most streams parallel the bank. Fishermen love to watch the water for any working fish that might be present. Because the banks themselves are often higher than the stream, observation is easy, not just for the angler, but—you guessed it—for the trout, too. If a fisherman happens to be working a run or working a bank you are walking along, *give him a wide berth by walking back and around his location.* Never allow yourself to become visible to the fish another angler is working, for you will surely spook those fish.

Walking or standing on the bank near where another angler is fishing also shows bad manners. Here, the bankside angler's high profile will put fish down.

Private water should also be respected by the fly fisherman. Always ask permission for access rather than operating on the assumption that all fish are public and therefore the land surrounding belongs to the public as well. Once you have received permission, be sure to close fences after entering and see that they are secure. Do not litter or disrupt crops or habitats. *Respect people's property as you would hope they would respect yours.*

Landing and playing fish also has its set of rules. In most cases, the angler who has hooked a fish has the right of way throughout a stream. If an angler has a running fish and needs to pass through your area, let him do so. Reel up and either step back to the bank or remain stationary and allow him to go around you. Also, never take the responsibility of landing another man's trout unless you are asked to assist; it can end in disaster. Even if the angler asks for help, give it willingly but proceed with caution: Your mistake could cause great disappointment and frustration to your fellow fisherman.

The above does not cover all the myriad streamside problems that may occur, just the most common ones. The manner in which we conduct ourselves on the various fishing waters is obviously as important as how we fish them. Etiquette, although it does not carry the force of law, or even regulation, is fundamental to the sport of fly fishing. And coupled with our attitude toward the fish and their environment, our manners become perhaps the most important aspect of the sport. The very future and livelihood of our sport depends on each of us and how we act, whatever our level of ability or our method.

CONSERVATION PROBLEMS AND ETHICS

Perhaps the greatest challenge facing fishermen, both today and in the future, is preserving the water systems that make the sport possible. Simply stated, if there is not adequate water for fish to thrive, all fishing, fly fishing included, will be impossible. Every fisherman must, therefore, concern himself with the precious environment in which fish are born, survive, and perpetuate themselves.

Up until the 1970s, the word "conservation" had only a dictionary meaning for most of us. Often, the manipulation of natural resources was governed by complacency and greed. Each bred an attitude that, in effect, said if one water resource became non-productive there would always be others to take its place. Well, I'm saddened to report that we are slowly running out of fishable systems. If we are not careful we will destroy what is left.

Industry has undeniably brought great wealth to individuals and to the nation. But, sadly, in too many instances, it has degraded most waterways it has touched. Streams that flowed through industrialized areas were often regarded either as highways, or as repositories for waste—everything from toxic chemicals to sewage—that affects not only the fish but the entire aquatic ecology. Poor forestry practices, particularly clearcutting, have caused erosion, clogging our streams and creeks with silt that renders them totally unsuitable for spawning or fish life.

Man has also taken it upon himself to divert the flow of our rivers to his own purposes. Hydroelectric dams, while providing cheap energy to the masses and irrigation to the farmer, have, in many cases, totally eliminated migratory runs of salmon and steelhead that existed in abundance just a few decades ago. Little thought was given to fish when the dam-building craze was at its height. Inadequate or nonexistent fish ladders were the norm, and nitrogen supersaturation at the base of the spillways, caused by the plunging water, was never anticipated. Granted, some dams have also provided fabulous tail race trout fisheries below the dams, but for the most part, dams have brought more harm than good. Only in recent years have the problems caused by dams been addressed, and largely through the efforts of fishermen will future runs of migratory fish survive.

It was once thought that the reservoirs created by dams would provide an endless supply of recreational resources, but they quickly developed into storage facilities for silt or toxic wastes, altering the complete ecology of the water. Yes, there was and is fishing in these impoundments, but biologists today concede that it is only a matter of time before many become useless for fish and recreational fishing.

Diverting rivers causes as many problems as harnessing their energy. It seems that every lover of the outdoors wants his little cabin in the woods beside a stream, but he does not want that friendly little river to turn on him and flood. To protect his property and investment, he "rip-raps"—channels the course of the river away from his private domain. This seemingly sensible precaution robs the fish of vital habitats. What was once a meandering river system, providing adequate habitat and holding water for fish, quickly turns into a velocity shoot, transferring water from Point A to Point B as quickly as possible. Little is left in these stretches for the fish to survive in.

Some of these intolerable conditions and hardships perpetrated by man on fish were done with high purpose and nothing but the best of intentions—except they backfired. Through ignorance, for many years fishermen, as well as various fish and game management personnel, felt that wild fish populations, once

Hatchery Fish

Hatchery fish are raised in great quantities and in a congested environment unlike that of natural streams.

Hand-fed through most of their lives, hatchery fish tend to have difficulty adapting to natural feeding. Consequently, when introduced to streams, many die within a short period of time.

depleted, could easily and simply be replaced through massive introductions of hatchery-raised species. At the turn of the century, fish culturists distributed various species that did help populate river systems with good variety. But after World War II, when fishing popularity increased and wild fish populations rapidly diminished, sportsmen clamored for more fish. Planting was thought to be the solution to the problem. Unfortunately, many of the same well-intentioned officials who were responsible for the ambitious planting programs have recently discovered how destructive hatchery-raised fish can be to the productivity of the river systems.

In one very important Montana Fish and Game study, conducted on the Madison River in the early 70s, the truth about supplementation came to light. First, hatchery fish were seen to have a very high mortality rate when introduced into the natural environment. Because they had been hand-fed in the hatchery to a catchable size, many simply were not able to adapt to the competitive wild environment. Also, it was discovered that when hatchery fish were introduced in great numbers to a particular river location, they tended to drive out the otherwise territorial resident wild trout. The overall effect was that the planted fish died, the wild fish disappeared, and a small fish population remained in the river. What little population remained to spawn turned out to be a breed greatly inferior to those that had originally existed.

Fishery management people also dabbled in the genetic structure of trout, looking for a fish capable of maturing very rapidly, obtaining a uniform size, and even spawning at different times of the year for easier management within the concrete raceways of the hatcheries. The result was a genetically inferior species that, although easily reared, no longer attained uniform growth but took on a girthless, snakelike profile.

Again, creating problems of these kinds was not the intention of those involved. In their enthusiasm for enhancing our fisheries, few foresaw the end results. Certainly, in the early stages of fishery experimentation, there was no way of knowing that crossing various genetic strains of fish would produce weaklings. But now there is a scientific basis for understanding these phenomena and many state programs are moving to rectify the situation, by reducing hatchery planting and watching more closely the genetic structure of the fish.

In all fairness to hatchery programs, it should be noted that, although they can have serious negative side effects in a wild trout fishery, there are waterways and impoundments that would be completely devoid of fish were it not for these programs. Lake systems that freeze solid during the winter, become excessively warm in summer, or have a limited capacity to perpetuate fish populations need to be planted. Also, because most states have different water types, containing

A necessary sign of the times.

varying degrees of temperature ranges, were it not for introduction programs, a full array of both cold and warm water species would not exist.

Hatcheries *do* have their place, but for the fly fisherman of today and the future it is obvious that some type of catch-and-release or restricted kill regulations, accompanied by more enlightened attitudes, is vitally necessary if we are to have fish of any consequence in years to come.

It is a fact that we are not living in an era that existed 50 or 100 years ago. Today, because of excessive fishing pressure, we can no longer live with the idea that we are entitled to an unlimited supply of fish. As my good friend Jack Hemingway stated and is often quoted, "It is not the responsibility of state fish and game commissions and agencies to supply protein to the fishing public." We know that the fish and game departments have tried to rectify a bad situation by supplementation, but we also know now that those efforts, however well intentioned, are detrimental to the water systems in the long run. More and more states are beginning to recognize that catch-and-release regulations have positive effects on both the fisheries and the fishermen. Today, those areas with highly restrictive regulations often produce not only substantial quantities of fish, but large, quality individuals as well. Fishermen quickly see the difference and gravitate to these areas, recognizing that where fish are plentiful and smart, there is more sport and more pleasure. Your consideration is also needed.

Even with catch-and-release regulations to guide us, the fish are still threatened unless we pay close attention to the manner in which we handle and release them. Most fish, especially trout, are fragile and cannot withstand excessive abuse at the hands of a fisherman. The slightest loss of blood or mild overexertion from overplaying can be lethal. Therefore, when hooking, playing, landing, and releasing fish, we must take care to minimize any damage. Barbless hooks are always a good idea, since they are easily removed without tearing the jaw or drawing blood. Also, instead of shotputting a fish back to the water, it is very important to hold it for a few moments facing upstream and move it back and forth, allowing it to get needed oxygen back into its bloodstream, and thus ensuring its survival.

How we regard and handle the environment in which fish live is our biggest challenge for the future. You may live in an area that is relatively free of environmental problems, but don't be complacent. What becomes deplorable in one part of the country can, and will, reach you as well. Regardless of where and how problems exist, we must all get involved if we are to save the life-giving water and fish habitat that we presently have. It cannot be the other person's fight. If we are to have fishing for our children and our children's children, we must all take a stand against those practices, organizations, and people that bring destruction to our water systems. It is simply up to all of us.

15

Fly Tying

While it is not essential for successful fly fishing that one learns how to tie flies, the skill certainly does enhance the sport. Fly tying knowledge enables you to understand the principles of the fly's construction, allowing you to be creative and free of reliance on others. Leaving to someone else the important task of designing a fly for your specific fishing situations always has drawbacks. Because certain materials react differently in certain types of water, it is inevitably necessary for the person on the stream to understand what causes a fly to do what it is intended to do. For example, wet flies are tied to sink and dry flies are tied to float. The materials used, naturally, differ, and, if you can't recognize the difference, you will never take that final step in reaching expert status.

So huge an array of materials, tools, hooks, threads, and hackles is on the market today that I cannot deal with them all here. If you are interested in tying, I urge you to seek out fly tying classes or ask for the advice of those who are already tying their own flies. Also, there are a great many books available (see page 254), and acquiring a good one will relieve you of the burden of commiting everything you learn to memory. Tools and materials can be purchased individually, but for those just beginning I highly recommend one of the many kits available from the mail order or retail outlets. From that base, you can continue to add to your collection from the endless supply of materials on the market.

Again, there are numerous fly tying procedures, and this book cannot present them all. However, the accompanying pictures should give you an understanding of how the basic flies are constructed. Regardless of what type you tie, you should always follow these general rules:

235

Simple fly-tying equipment allows you to create your
own imitations of the foods that fish feed upon.

1. When placing the hook in the vise, never bury the barb completely in the jaws. This can fracture the very fine point and ruin all your efforts.

2. Fly construction generally begins at the bend of the hook and ends above the eye.

3. All materials used for the fly are tied in first with the thread always staying ahead of the materials so that the material can be tied off.

4. Always leave room at the eye of the hook so the fly can be tied off.

Tying a Fly

One of the easiest flies to tie (and, thus, one you should start with as a novice) is the Woolly Worm. To start, place the hook in a vise, making sure to expose the barb slightly. If you wish to weight the fly, wrap a few turns of lead wire around the hook's shank and secure the wire with a few turns of thread.

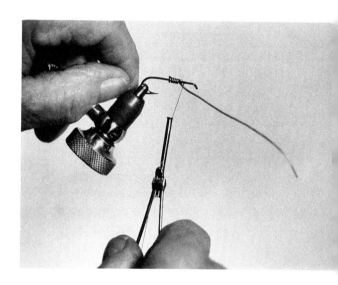

Trim the excess wire and wrap thread over the shank of the hook, giving a good base for the materials to follow. The thread should now be positioned at the bend of the hook.

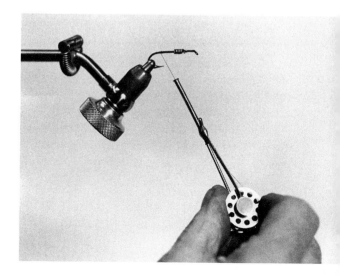

Tie in the tail material and trim excess fibers. Note: Most flies, like the Woolly Worm, are tied, starting from the bend and moving toward the eye of the hook.

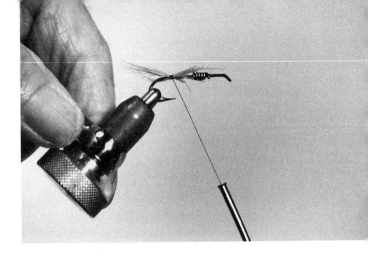

Now tie in all material necessary to complete the fly—in this case, grizzly hackle and chenille. Wind thread toward eye of the hook.

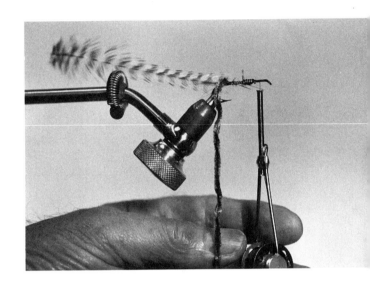

Wrap the chenille evenly, so that the wraps just touch each other, up the hook shank and tie off with a few wraps of thread. Leave room near the eye of the hook, in order, later, to form a nice head.

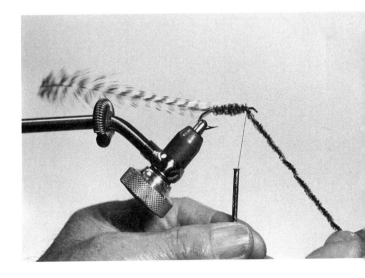

Wrap hackle,
evenly-spaced, over the
chenille and toward the
eye, and tie off. This style
of hackle wrapping is
known as "palmering".

With the thread, form a
nice, tapered head above
the eye.

Using a whip finish tool,
tie off the fly. You should
also learn to tie the whip
finish knot with your
hands.

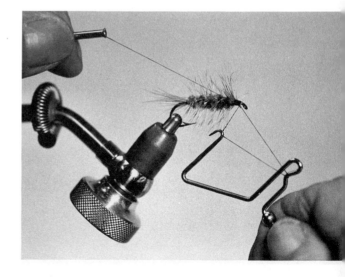

Now apply two or three drops of head cement.

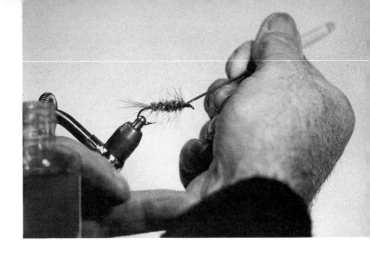

And, voila! Your finished fly!

FLY TYING PROCEDURE

Although the basic rule of thumb is that you work from the bend of the hook to the eye, there are a few deviations from this that must be understood in completing the fly. The following list outlines the basic sequence we follow in applying the materials to the hook for different fly types.

Dry Fly—Tail, wing, body, hackle.
Nymph—Tail, body, ribbing (if any) which is sometimes wound over the body material, wing case, thorax, legs.
Wet Fly/Streamer—Tail, body, ribbing (if any), hackle*, wing.

---

*In some streamers, hackle is applied after the wing emplacement.

16

Accessories

Many people jokingly have said that the great draw of fly fishing is not necessarily the method itself but all the tools and gadgets that go along with the sport. I, for one, can't deny this, for the sport does have a seemingly endless array of paraphernalia that, sad to say, we seem not to be able to live without. Each year manufacturers both large and small dream up new and helpful items. Although none is absolutely required for catching fish, most add to the convenience of our time spent on the streams. The following is a discussion of those items that can aid any fisherman.

FISHING VESTS

For consolidating and organizing the immense number of items that we use, the fishing vest is certainly the most convenient container of all. Vests come in many designs and price ranges. Most have a seemingly staggering number of pockets, each of which is fashioned to fit one of the various types of fly boxes, bottles, and miscellaneous packages that the fisherman carries to a stream. Both regular and short lengths are available, with the latter being very popular for wading in deep water. Regardless of your choice of design, it is important to acquire one that fits your needs and will withstand many years of use, for a fishing vest is an essential item for fly fishermen.

ACCESSORIES

Each tool that goes into or attaches on a vest is designed for specific functions, and there will be times when you will need all the accessories.

241

With its wide assortment of pockets and pouches, the fishing vest is the angler's traveling toolbox.

Scissors

As far as I am concerned, a pair of sharp scissors is the most important cutting tool you can carry. It is useful not only for cutting leader but also for trimming and reshaping flies.

Needlenose Pliers

Today many trout streams have barbless-hook regulations, and, because many purchased flies do not come barbless, a good pair of small needlenose pliers is needed for flattening the barb. In purchasing pliers, make sure the inside jaws are flat and smooth, not serrated.

Surgical Forceps

Surgical forceps, or hemostats, are essential for disengaging a fly from the fish's mouth. Available in both curved and straight tips, they protect the fly from being mangled by fingers, and, with their locking feature, they can be hung from a vest pocket flap for easy accessibility.

Clippers

Clippers have long been used to trim and cut excess leader materials. Although a useful and inexpensive item, their disadvantage is that they are often not sharp enough for every task, which can make them ineffective for trimming and reshaping flies. If a pair of good scissors is not available, nail clippers of one type or another are your best bet.

Retrievits

Retrievits, or pin-on reels, are a convenient way of holding the various tools. The retractable cord attached to the vest keeps the tools, when not in use, conveniently close. A very handy item.

Leader Straighteners

I am not a great fan of leader straighteners, if for no other reason than that they are generally used improperly. Most contain a rubber backing, which, when the leader is pulled through, will straighten out its memory coils. Unfortunately, the rubber can build up heat friction, which weakens the leaders. If you do use a straightener, be sure to wet it before you strip the leader through it.

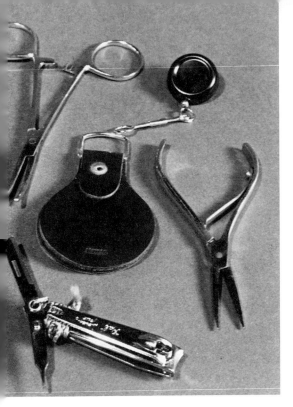

Accessories.
You don't necessarily need every accessory shown here, but each can be handy in a pinch.

Sunglasses.
A good pair of polarized sunglasses are essential to the fly fisherman. Not only do they protect the eyes from stray flies, their polarization cuts glare, enabling a better view of both fly and fish.

Tippet Dispenser

Since fly fishermen need to carry tippet material of different diameters, I recommend a dispenser to organize the tippet spools. Dispensers are fashioned so that the tippet of the appropriate size can be quickly located and individual spools do not unravel in your vest pocket. Although not essential, they are convenient.

Sunglasses

Polarized sunglasses are the most important single accessory a fisherman should possess. They not only cut the glare off the water, enabling you to see both fly and fish, they protect the eyes from a stray cast of the deadly barbed hook. Years ago, because of the nature of polarization in sunglasses, many were made of soft plastics, which had a tendency both to distort vision and to scratch easily. But today's hard plastics have made polarized glasses durable and optically correct at nominal prices. Get the best you can afford. Your eyes will love you.

Sprays and ointments.
Smart anglers always carry special sprays and pastes to: 1) help dry flies stay afloat, 2) help leaders sink.

SPRAYS AND OINTMENTS

Dry Fly Sprays and Pastes

If you intend to fish a dry fly, a silicon-based dry fly spray or paste-type ointment will help keep the fly floating. The paste type lasts a bit longer on the fly than do the sprays. In purchasing dry fly ointments, look for those that are colorless and odorless.

Dry Fly Powders

Relatively new on the market, dry fly powders have replaced the once-popular Amadu fungus for cleaning and drying a dry fly. Dry fly powders remove mucous that the fly picks up from the fish's mouth, and, because they have a silicon base, will contribute to fly flotation as well.

Leader Sinks

Although not essential, leader sinks aid in breaking the surface film, allowing the leader to drift below surface, where it is best disguised. Fishermen once used Lava soap and mud from the streambank to accomplish this task, but today, the various commercial leader sink dressings are both convenient and effective.

Insect Repellents

Regardless of where you fish, various kinds of biting insects are likely to be present. A good insect repellent is therefore essential. When using and applying repellent, it is important to keep your hands clean of it, as the various chemicals used can be destructive of fly lines and rod finishes, and the petrol odors are detectable to fish.

FLY BOXES, BOOKS, AND WALLETS

A complete fisherman should carry an assortment of flies, and these important items need to be conveniently stored for easy accessibility and selection. Fly boxes thus become part of the basic gear of a fly fisherman. Boxes come in a variety of sizes, shapes, styles, and materials and are designed not only to store sufficient quantities of imitations but to fit in the various pockets of our vests.

Plastic-Compartment Boxes

Unbreakable plastic boxes are the most popular type of fly container available today. Inexpensive and very rugged, they come in compartment configurations designed for the various imitations you may use. If there is one disadvantage to the compartment box, it's that the actual fly selection and identification can be difficult, especially if many flies are carried. Plastic boxes *with foam inserts* to which the fly hook can be firmly attached facilitate better organization and easier recognition.

Metal Boxes

Metal boxes have been around for many years and are still a convenient way to carry your flies. Some come with clips designed primarily for wet flies and nymphs; others have coil springs into which the hook is inserted; still others have individual compartments with small windows so that you can see the fly

Fly Boxes

Fly-box designs, styles, and functions are numerous. Some come with various compartments, others with foam or magnetic pads, in materials ranging from metal to plastic. Here, the author's fly boxes: one for each stream and pattern type, with foam pads for easy inventory.

but it cannot fall out. Metal boxes are generally heavy and, I have found, do have a tendency to rust hooks, especially after the box has taken the inevitable dunking in the stream. Window-type containers also have a tendency to pop open when the box itself has been unlatched.

Fly Books

Zippered fly books are primarily used for wet flies and streamers. Generally constructed of leather with a shearling fleece lining to which the flies are attached, they are a reliable way to store the often-valuable flies.

Fleece Patches and Hatbands

Although fleece patches come standard on vests and are convenient for storing flies, I do not recommend their use. In general, they lose more flies than they store. I often refer to them as "the fly retailer's dream," because they guarantee that the fisherman will return to the store to replace those flies he lost using these "conveniences."

Leader Wallets

Because leaders come in a variety of lengths and sizes, leader wallets are helpful for storing and sorting the assortment of fly leaders that we must carry. They fit nicely into vest pockets, and I highly recommend them for overall storage.

WADING GEAR

Next to rod, reel, and line, wading gear is perhaps the costliest—but at the same time the most important—piece of equipment you will buy. As a small boy, I waded the streams wet, with only tennis shoes and long pants. It was not until I donned my first pair of waders that I realized the comfort I had been missing.

Waders have come a long way in the past years, but still no one manufacturer has made the perfect, indestructible product. All waders will rip on a barbed-wire fence but, mirabile dictu, *most* are easily repaired. Because they need to be water-impermeable and are designed to fit the average fisherman (and many question what that is), wading gear can be excessively hot and not necessarily form-fitting. Regardless of these faults, it does keep us dry and protect us from the bone-chilling cold of many trout waters, making it an essential item.

Waders come in a variety of styles and materials, all of which have their advantages and disadvantages. Let's take a look at some of the basic types.

Hip and Chest, Boot-Foot Wader

For years, the hip boot and full chest wader have been the most popular type of wading gear used by fishermen. Manufactured as a single unit, with the boot attached to the upper wader, hip and chest waders are designed not only to protect you from the elements but also for convenient donning and removal. The hip boot, which rises to about crotch level, is used for fishing small streams and wading in waters that are not deep. The chest-high type, extending to the chest or armpits, is for wading deeper water, and overall is the most utilized style.

As popular as these two types of waders are, they do have their disadvantages. Because they are designed for the average body size, they have a tendency to be either baggy or tight-fitting, especially respective to the leg length, or rise. The latter, although not a problem with hip boots, can be quite uncomfortable in the chest-high type. Also, because the shoe portion of the wader is constructed of rubber and is oversized, it does not offer good support for general walking and wading freestone streams.

Stockingfoot Waders

For years stockingfoot waders were used primarily by those fishermen who ventured into fast, heavy-water streams, for they offered greater support than did the boot-foot type. Today their popularity, especially among fly fishermen, has surpassed the traditional type wader because of function, wading support, overall utility, and longevity. They come in a wide variety of materials that are lightweight, flexible, and warm.

The stockingfoot is a full chest wader, but instead of having a rubber boot attached it relies on a leather or synthetic wading shoe placed over the foot portion: hence their descriptive name. Most stockingfoot waders are made of latex rubber or a coated nylon material, either of which is very serviceable for fishing. In addition, neoprene rubber waders have more recently become very popular. The material offers tremendous flexibility and uniform insulating value resulting in protection from bone-chilling waters. Too, because it seals against the outside temperature on hot days, the neoprene will not allow you to get any warmer than your normal body temperature.

Wading Shoes

Placed over the stockingfoot wader is a wading shoe, which today comes in a variety of styles and materials designed to give you support for walking. Years ago most wading shoes were made of leather, but today many are synthetic imitations of leather, which can withstand watery situations without rotting. Some are nothing more than an advanced copy of a high top tennis shoe with a hard sole and toe to protect the feet from sharp rocks. Others resemble a working boot that offers good ankle support and added protection. Because most fall roughly in the same price range, I suggest the latter, full-lace type.

Gravel and small rocks are always a problem with stockingfoot waders,

Waders

A

B

C

D

For shallow-stream wading, hip boots (A) may do the job, but chest waders (B) and neoprene stocking-foot waders (C), are more versatile. Top your stocking-foot waders with a pair of felt-soled wading boots and gravel guards (D), and with any wader, follow the example of these anglers: wear a belt.

and many fishermen purchase various types of gravel guards. Wrapped around the top portion of the wading shoe, they keep the small annoyances from trickling down against the feet and ankles. No matter which type of stocking-foot wader you choose, be sure to include a pair of gravel guards with them.

Wading Cleats

Whether you choose boot or stockingfoot waders, it is imperative that the waders and wading shoes have felt soles to help prevent slippage on rocks. Sometimes even more traction is desirable. Wading cleats, with aluminum grid bars in various configurations, attached to the bottom of the boot or wading shoe, counter the most slippery conditions. The most popular are the galoshes-type that slip over the boot. Some manufacturers also offer a sandal-type cleat with protruding spikes, useful where the rock is very porous. For the common, rounded river rocks, the grid-bar design seems to work best.

MISCELLANEOUS ITEMS

There are always a few items that may not be essential but do add to the convenience and comfort of fishing. Some of them, I think, should be at least considered by the well-prepared angler.

Long Underwear

Regardless of where you wade, long underwear can make the experience more comfortable. If you do a great deal of fishing, you must keep your legs as warm as possible, for over the years the cold water will take its toll on your circulation. A good set of underwear, made from either a combination of wool and cotton or one of the new polypropylene materials that wick moisture away from the skin, will do the job nicely. To help avoid crippling leg pain in later in life, wear long underwear.

Raingear

Adequate raingear is one of the more important things a fisherman can carry, for you never know when a sudden rainstorm will appear. Raingear comes in a variety of materials, from rubberized nylon to synthetic-coated stock. Rubberized nylon, although it does not offer "breathability," still works the best. It protects you not only from a quick shower, but also from a day-long rain, which eventually will penetrate any other types of materials. Because it lacks breathability, inside condensation does occur and can make things rather clammy if you have to wear it for a long time. The new synthetic materials, with their "breathability" that allows water vapor to escape through the fabric, have taken the outdoors world by storm, but you should recognize the difference between these highly *water-resistant* materials and those that are *waterproof.* Although breathable, water-resistant synthetics work for most rainy conditions, a torrential all-day rain will eventually cause them to absorb water and leak.

When you purchase raingear, make sure that the seams are stitched, that zippers are rugged, and that the material will withstand years of punishment. Workmanship is important. And remember, raingear belongs with the fisherman, in his vest, while fishing; it does not belong in the car or at the house, where it will do absolutely no good in the event of a quick downpour. Also, even if rain is not imminent, it may come in handy as a windbreak if the weather turns chilly.

Rodbags and Luggage

There is a full range of products available for carrying gear and personal items on a trip or to the stream. Medium and large duffels are nice because they can carry all your wading gear, vests, nets, and so forth, in addition to your clothing. A small kit or shoulder bag for carrying the essential equipment that won't fit in vests (such as reels, extra spools and fly boxes, wading patch kits and other accessories) also has its place.

Rod bags are not essential but they keep all your rods conveniently together in one place and prevent them from banging around in the back seat of a car. A bag and crushproof metal carrying tube are, however, absolutely essential for transporting each of your rods on long trips.

Appendix:
Reading

This book is designed to be a general reference for the beginning and intermediate angler. I cannot delve into every subject, but other books are available that discuss the various aspects of the sport in more detail. The following books are some that I feel should be part of any serious fly fisherman's library.

General Reading

Brooks, Joe. 1972. *Trout Fishing,* New York: Outdoor Life, Harper & Row.
Published in the early '70s, this is still a very good general book on fly fishing for trout. A book I often recommend to beginning anglers.

McClane, Al. 1965. *McClane's New Standard Fishing Encyclopedia.* New York: Holt Rinehart & Winston.
A fabulous book, recommended for any library. Contains a wealth of information on all types of fishing, fisheries, and fish.

Schwiebert, Ernest. 1978. *Trout.* New York: E.P. Dutton.
Incredible two-volume work of some 1,700 pages. It very possibly is the most comprehensive book in print on the subject of fly fishing for trout. Particularly good for its historical information.

Fly Entomology

Arbona, Fred, Jr. 1980. *Mayflies, the Angler and the Trout.* New York: Winchester Press.
One of the latest and most important works on the mayfly, it answers many questions that previous works left open. Particularly good for those wishing to learn the keying out process for the various species. Essential for the serious angler.

Caucci, Al; Nastasi, Bob. 1975. *Hatches.* New York: Compara Hatch Ltd.
Another good book dealing with the mayfly. Good color photos. It describes in detail many of the important hatches, particularly in the East and Midwest. Also deals with specific fly imitations.

LaFontaine, Gary. 1981. *Caddisflies.* New York: Nick Lyons Books.
Not many books on the caddisfly have been published, and certainly this is the most definitive work. Essential for those anglers wishing to understand more about this very important food source of fish.

Marinaro, Vincent. 1970. *Modern Dry Fly Code,* New York: Crown.
Although first published in 1950, this is still one of the great books when it comes to describing the importance of fly silhouette, the trout's window, and the creation of the thorax-style fly. Many consider it a classic.

Schwiebert, Ernest. 1955. *Matching the Hatch.* New York: Macmillan.
This was one of the very first fully comprehensive books on the various hatches and food sources throughout the country and not just in specific areas. Although more recent works have altered some of Ernie's original findings, it is still considered a classic among fly fishing reference books.

Swisher, Doug; Richards, Carl. 1971. *Selective Trout.* New York: Crown.
Opened the entomologist era of the '70s. One of the classic reference materials describing the selectivity of trout, the cycle of mayflies, important hatches throughout the United States, and, most important, fly styles (namely the no-hackles) for highly selective fish. Highly recommended.

Swisher, Doug; Richards, Carl; Arbona, Fred, Jr. 1980 *Stoneflies.* New York: Nick Lyons Books.
Like the caddisfly, stoneflies have been the subject of very few books. This one is perhaps the best. Highly recommended for the angler who wishes to complete his reference material on one of the three most important food sources of fish.

Whitlock, Dave. 1982. *Guide to Aquatic Trout Foods.* New York: Nick Lyons Books.
A good, general work describing all types of food that fish feed upon. Wonderfully illustrated. It gives the general angler opportunities to understand what is available in all of our water systems.

Fly Tying

Bay, Kenneth. 1970. *How to Tie Freshwater Flies.* New York: Winchester Press.
There have been many books written on the subject of fly tying, most of which are very good. Ken's book is an excellent reference for those learning to tie the basics, including dries, wets, nymphs, and streamers.

Dennis, Jack. 1974. *Western Fly Tying Manual.* 2 vol. Jackson Hole, WY: Snake River Books.
A good book for those wishing to learn the western type of tying, particularly hairwing type flies.

Leiser, Eric. 1977. *Complete Book of Fly Tying.* New York: Alfred Knopf.
Not only does Eric describe in detail the method of tying many flies, but he is particularly good in explaining the various types of tools, materials, hooks, and even dyeing processes that are used.

Miscellaneous Reading

Brooks, Charles. 1976. *Nymph Fishing for Larger Trout.* New York: Crown.
This book is particularly good for those wishing to learn good, solid nymph techniques. It is oriented toward all nymph fishing, but especially that of the West.

Hills, John Waller. 1971. *A History of Fly Fishing for Trout.* New York: Freshet Press.
For those who want to learn more of the history of the sport, this is a very good book.

Kreh, Lefty. 1974. *Fly Fishing in Salt Water.* New York: Crown.
A good, basic book for those anglers wishing to gain further knowledge and understanding of fly fishing for fish in salt water. Lefty certainly shows his expertise in explaining the basics of this environment. A very important reference material.

Kreh, Lefty; Sosin, Mark. 1972. *Practical Knots.* New York: Crown.
Besides the basic knots, this how-to book describes and explains the wide variety of knots used by all fishermen. Because knots are an important element in the line-to-fly link, this is an almost essential reference volume on the subject.

Livingston, A.D. 1976. *Flyrodding for Bass.* Philadelphia and New York: Lippincott.
More and more books on fly fishing for bass and panfish are appearing, and this book deals with the subject as well as any other on the market. I highly recommend it for those who wish to pursue these great fish with a fly rod.

Schwiebert, Ernest. 1973. *Nymphs.* New York: Winchester Press.
Although rather specific in nature, this becomes a good reference for those anglers wishing to recognize the underwater stages of all the various types of insects available to the freshwater fish. The color plates are magnificent and can be used as a reference for fly tying.

Also: Anything written by Gene Hill. Although Gene's books are not meant to be how-to guides, Gene may be one of the great outdoor writers of our time. He will make you laugh, move you to cry, and prompt you to reminisce. His thoughtfulness and insight stand out.

National Organizations and Magazines

Federation of Fly Fishermen, PO Box 1088, West Yellowstone, MT 59758. Many local clubs nationwide. Write for the one nearest you.

Trout Unlimited, PO Box 992, Taunton, MA 02780. Publishers of *Trout* magazine. Many local chapters. Write for the one nearest you.

International Game Fish Association, 3000 East Los Aloas Blvd., Fort Lauderdale, FL 33316. World Records.

Nature Conservancy, Silver Creek Preserve, Box 624, Picabo, ID 83348. One of the finest environmental organizations operating today.

Fly Fisherman Magazine, Historial Times Inc., Box 8200, Harrisburg, PA 17105.

Rod and Reel Magazine, Box 370, Camden, ME 04843.